STRESS SUCKS!

A Girl's Guide to Managing School, Friends and Life

Roni Cohen Sandler, Ph.D.

Connecticut • New York • Colorado

Table of Contents

Other Books by Roni Cohen Sandler, Ph.D. v

STRESS SUCKS!

CHAPTER ONE
Too Much Pressure! 1

CHAPTER TWO
Where Stress Comes From 12

CHAPTER THREE
How Stress Kills Success 24

CHAPTER FOUR
Failure is Your Friend (& Other Attitude Adjustments) 31

CHAPTER FIVE
Taking Care of You 38

CHAPTER SIX
Work Habits that Work for You 48

CHAPTER SEVEN
Distracted By Problems 58

CHAPTER EIGHT
The College Process—Myths, Truths, and Strategies 65

APPENDIX
De-Stressing Your School Environment 79

Copyright Notices

Roni Cohen Sandler, Ph.D.

STRESS SUCKS!
A Girl's Guide to Managing School, Friends, and Life

Copyright © 2013 by Roni Cohen Sandler, Ph.D.

Int'l ISBN: 978-1-62071-130-9
ISBN: 1-62071-130-3

All rights reserved. Except for use in any review, the reproduction or utilization of this work in whole or in part in any form by any electronic means is not cool with us unless written permission has been received from the publisher

For information address:
Author & Company, LLC
P.O. Box 291
Cheshire, CT 06410-9998

This book was designed by iLN™
and manufactured in the United States of America.

Other Books by
Roni Cohen Sandler, Ph.D.

Easing Their Stress:
Helping Our Girls Thrive in the Age of Pressure

I'm Not Mad, I Just Hate You:
A New Understanding of Mother-Daughter Conflict

"Trust Me, Mom"
A Less Stressful Approach to Mothering Teenage Daughters

To learn more about Roni Cohen-Sandler and
all of her books please visit:

http://www.ronicohensandler.com

STRESS SUCKS!

CHAPTER ONE

Too Much Pressure!

"I think that there is soooo much pressure for girls to be perfect. You have the media with all those super skinny girls with perfect hair and makeup and clothes, and you have those snotty girls in school that tease you if you don't wear what they wear, and parents and teachers always nagging on us to do better in school. It's hard to keep up with all of the pressure. I feel like there is so much expected of me with my friends, family, teachers, and coaches, it's terrible." —Brittany

As a teen girl, you're part of an extraordinary group that's slowly but surely changing the world. When Google held their first annual National Science Fair, which drew 10,000 students from 91 countries, who do you think won all of the age categories? You guessed it: girls. And when high school students recently traveled to Washington, D.C. to hand-deliver an online petition with 118,000 signatures calling for a woman to moderate the 2012 presidential debates, of course those three students were three determined girls. These days, not only are teen girls accomplishing amazing things, but you're also pretty much leaving guys in the dust.

The facts couldn't be clearer. From kindergarten on, girls are better students. In high school, you get better grades in every subject and have higher GPAs and class ranks than boys. You're more likely to take AP classes and to get higher scores on standardized reading and writing tests. While boys still have the edge on math and science tests, you're closing the gap there, too. This may be hard to believe, but more of you are even signing up for the *hardest* math classes! Beyond academics, girls rule in high school. You're more likely to work on the school paper or yearbook and to hold offices in student government. Far more of you are also going on to college; in hundreds of universities, the female to male ratio is now 60-40.

"So What's the Problem?"

This sounds awesome, right? It is awesome. But, unfortunately, there's a downside to all this success. Along the way, girls are paying a huge price.

As a psychologist, I hear teen girls everywhere—in my office, in emails, at schools all around the US and Canada—describing unbearable pressures. Many of you want to excel not just in a few things, but in absolutely everything. You think that to be successful today you have to be extraordinary. As *Christa* says, *"Girls always feel like we're not good enough for society. We're being pressured into being sporty, smart, pretty, and popular. Why can't we just be a little good at all these things? Why do we have to be great at everything? No wonder so many teen girls have problems."*

Can you relate? Do you hope to ace your tests, star in sports, be popular, shine in your extracurricular activities, make your parents and teachers proud, and get accepted to a good college—while also looking great and staying thin? Do you sometimes worry that you're not living up to expectations or that you're disappointing everyone—maybe even yourself?

Like many girls I speak to, *Lauren* describes feeling horrendous pressure—not just once in awhile, but every day: *"It seems like the homework never ends. You can never get ahead. You can only stop yourself from falling behind. All I do every weekend is sit at home in my room and do my homework. I don't have time to go out or even relax."* With this sort of grueling schedule, girls feel as if they're going through their lives on autopilot, barely able to keep up and not feeling good about anything they're doing.

Here's the problem: constant stress, hectic schedules, and mind-numbing fatigue weigh you down, making it even harder to cope. When you're worn out by lack of sleep, seemingly unending piles of homework, drama in your social life, and demanding parents, teachers, or coaches, even a regular day can become a total nightmare. Little frustrations, annoyances, and disappointments that normally wouldn't be a big deal somehow add up and seem completely overwhelming.

Let's say you don't like your grade on a Social Studies test, your phys ed teacher yells at you for being late to class (even though it wasn't your fault!), and your BFF gives you the cold shoulder without a word of explanation. Suddenly, you feel like you're about to burst into tears or have a complete meltdown. This is how stress gets to you. Whether it sneaks up or attacks as quickly and fiercely as a summer thunderstorm, it can make you feel utterly hopeless and helpless. Here's how *Kai* expressed it in an email:

> *"There's no way to explain all the stress. I'm more worried about grades every minute than learning the material. I can't get everything done and do it right. At night, I always stay awake thinking of all I have to do. Sometimes I wake up in the middle of the night and do it. There really aren't enough hours in the day. The stress is like falling down a big hole."*

Just How Stressed *Are* You?

Like many girls, you may think, "I'm way too stressed-out," "I'm completely exhausted" or "I'm totally overwhelmed." Or it may be hard to recognize that some changes or problems in your life are actually signs of too much stress. Right now, take a moment to check in with yourself to find out how all the pressure is affecting you.

The "Assess Your Stress" Quiz shown below can also be accessed on my Facebook page, so you don't have to do the math.

QUIZ: Assess Your Stress

Thinking about the past two months, how much do you agree with each of these statements? Circle your answers as follows:

1 = Not So Much   2 = Pretty Much   3 = Very Much

Statement	1	2	3
Learning isn't fun anymore	1	2	3
I wish I were a better student	1	2	3
I never get enough sleep	1	2	3
I have no time to read for pleasure	1	2	3
It's hard to turn off my brain to fall asleep	1	2	3
Thinking of the future worries me	1	2	3
I dread school	1	2	3
I skip meals or eat junk food on the go	1	2	3
I can't control things that happen	1	2	3
I feel cranky	1	2	3
I avoid speaking up in class	1	2	3
My parents and/or teachers expect too much of me	1	2	3
I get a lot of headaches, stomach aches, & muscle pains	1	2	3
I'm tempted to take Adderall or Ritalin to do better	1	2	3
Fitting in at school is my top priority	1	2	3
I get a lot of colds and viruses	1	2	3
Loading up on caffeine and/or sugar helps me stay awake	1	2	3
My teachers don't like me	1	2	3
I've been blowing off homework	1	2	3
Thinking about my problems makes it hard to concentrate	1	2	3
To let loose, I do risky things	1	2	3
I compare myself to my siblings, friends, or classmates	1	2	3
To avoid making trouble, I keep my feelings to myself	1	2	3
I've been having meltdowns and/or outbursts	1	2	3
Smoking, drinking, drugs, or sex gets my mind off things	1	2	3

25—41 (Calm Under Pressure)

Although you feel pressured at times (who doesn't?), for the most part you're managing well. Stress isn't causing major problems in your life right now. But make sure you're being honest with yourself and not ignoring symptoms just to keep pushing ahead. There's no shame in admitting when stress gets to you. Use the strategies in this book to restore serenity when pressure does spike (such as during crunch times) and to make your life even more balanced and fun.

42—58 (A Stress Mess)

You're definitely feeling too much pressure, but the good news is that you're savvy enough to realize you're struggling. Good for you for knowing yourself so well and trying to take better care of yourself before you get totally overwhelmed. As you keep reading and learning different techniques, check back with your stress level to decide which ones work best for you. Not only will life become calmer and easier, but also you'll have great coping skills for whatever challenges arise in the future.

59—75 (Whoa, Breathe!!!)

You're suffering from way, way too much stress and it's definitely causing big problems—but at least you know it and are ready to do something about it. That's the most important step. Although things may seem completely out of control sometimes, you have the power to significantly reduce the pressure. As you'll see, many girls who were just as stressed-out got huge relief. So can you! Think positively and be open to small changes that'll make you happier. You deserve that, so get started now!

It's a Scarier World

No matter how badly stress is affecting you, the first thing you should know is that you're not alone. Research shows stress has risen about 44% in the past 5 years, and 1/3 of young people in this country report stress-related physical symptoms. In many ways, growing up is harder now than it was when your parents were teenagers. In fact, with ever-increasing pressures to keep up, stand out, and find your talent at ever-younger ages, you're probably even more stressed-out than your older siblings were at your age.

With the crazy competition for college and internships, the economy, terrorism, so few job prospects for college graduates, and other problems adults are dealing with, it's not at all surprising that many parents these days are anxious to know their kids are doing okay. You probably sense this nervous energy whenever your parents ask about a test grade or suggest you take honors or AP classes or encourage you to try out for a special orchestra, leading role in the play, or spot on a premier sports team.

These accomplishments reassure them you're on the road to success. But what your parents consider "encouragement" may seem to you nonstop nagging or criticism. Their anxiety about your future probably shoots your own stress level through the roof.

Girl Stress

To learn more about the stress teen girls like you are experiencing, I surveyed nearly 3000 students in middle schools and high schools around the country. I also interviewed hundreds more girls, either once or during six-week focus groups. Since then, I've spoken to thousands of teen girls in assemblies, workshops, and small gatherings. Sometimes I also get to work with parents and teachers to educate them about how to reduce the stress you and girls everywhere are experiencing.

What I know for sure is that this has become a national epidemic. If you're in middle school or high school, most of you are feeling *too much* or *way too much* pressure to get good grades. Nearly 2/3 of you say you get *too much* or *way too much* homework. If you're in middle school now, almost 2/3 of you find you have *too little* or *not nearly enough* free time and 3/4 of you think that in high school. By middle school, more than 1/3 of you *usually* or *always* worry about getting into the "right" college. And by high school, twice as many of you agonize about where you'll be accepted.

I also learned that girls are more stressed-out than boys, who are generally less invested in school. You're 55% more likely than guys to put pressure on yourself to get good grades and do well in school. That's a *lot* of extra pressure! But it doesn't end there.

Girls and boys go about their school days totally differently. While guys focus on getting through and graduating, you probably care about every minute of every day. From homeroom to last period, you're probably taking stock of how well your relationships are going. Does your teacher seem pleased with your grade, class participation, or project? Did your best friend really give you a weird look in the hallway, or were you just being overly sensitive? Is she mad or dealing with a problem? If you sense something isn't quite right, you're likely to think (aka *obsess*) about it until you can figure it out or fix it.

This became crystal clear a few years back when I was seeing two teens in therapy. Both of their closest friends suddenly dropped them. Lucinda spent her sessions agonizing about what she possibly could have done to tick off her BFF, growing sadder and lonelier by the week. Tim said he didn't know why his best friend had stopped talking to him, but he seemed to take it more in stride. Thinking his calm approach might help Lucinda, I asked Tim how he handled the situation. First he looked at me as if I'd grown two heads. Then he shrugged and said, "I changed my lunch table." Problem solved. How simple is that?

There's another huge reason why girls stress more than boys: appearance. Can you imagine guys spending so much time assembling their outfits, getting their hair either perfectly straight or just curly enough, and putting on just the right amount of make-up? Let's face it, boys just don't have the intense pressures girls do to have flawless skin, the trendiest clothes, great accessories, and ideal hair. Like many girls, you too probably use valuable time and energy worrying about looking *too* something: too fat, too skinny, too babyish, too edgy, too nerdy, too sporty, too brainy, or too slutty. A freshman girl I know told her mother, "I just want to look normal enough so that people don't talk about me."

All these choices can make teen girls feel like they're walking tightropes. The path to success seems so narrow and treacherous that you fear one wrong step—a horrible grade, a stupid comment, an unfortunate fashion choice, a lost game—will topple you into an abyss of failure, along with all your future goals. Stress much?

Knowing how many other girls are suffering probably won't make you feel a whole lot better. But it may help keep your own stress in perspective. Too often, I hear girls say they're "the only ones who are stressed-out." As you look around and compare yourself to friends and classmates, it is easy to think you're the only one who's having trouble handling the pressure. This isn't even remotely true. What's worse, if you believe that, you'll start to think less of yourself. Negative thoughts eat away at self-confidence, actually *worsening* your ability to cope with everyday stresses. So not helpful!

Keeping Stress Hidden

What also makes it harder for girls to cope is that you usually hide your distress from teachers, parents, guidance counselors, and friends—in other words, the very people who can help. You may even hide your pain from yourself, denying how bad your stress is or how it's affecting you. Do you try to convince yourself that things aren't that terrible, that you should just suck it up, or that admitting to being overwhelmed would make you a total whiner? You might hesitate to speak up if you want to:

❋ **<u>Limit exposure.</u>** If you already feel like your parents are watching your every move, you may worry that revealing your stress would make them examine you under a microscope.

❋ **<u>Minimize micromanaging.</u>** If you admit to having trouble, might you suddenly find mom or dad monitoring every assignment, test grade, friendship, and game score? As *Holly* explains, *"Why would I want my parents to know when I screw up? Why do they need to know how stressed I am? If they get more freaked, then they'd just nag me more about my homework or make sure I'm not 'wasting time' online. That's all I need!"*

❋ **<u>Avoid extra work.</u>** Do you worry that 'fessing up to a less-than-stellar grade will make your parents hire more tutors, ground you on weekends, and take away what little down time you have?

❋ **<u>Not worsen parents' stress.</u>** If your mother and/or father are dealing with their own problems, you might try not to give them even more to worry about.

❋ **<u>Seem okay & successful.</u>** Do you think asking for help makes you look flawed or weak? *Lindsay* says, *"I guess I could talk to my teachers, but there's always that sense of intimidation. I don't want to be the one that 'complains.'"*

❋ **<u>Blend in.</u>** I've said this before, but it's worth repeating. If you think you're the only one feeling pressure or having a tough time coping, you're more likely to feel bad about yourself and keep quiet about it. But this only makes the problem worse.

Girls are such pros at hiding pain that many of your parents don't even know about it. I learned in my study that if you're among the most pressured teen girls, less than half of you think your parents realize just how stressed-out you are. You might in fact believe your mother or father wants you to be *more* pressured—which is horrifying! A recent survey by the American Psychological Association found that although stress is taking a toll on the health of teens and even younger children, parents aren't recognizing kids' physical symptoms as signs of stress.

Stress Should NOT Be a Given

These days, many people think you have to be stressed-out if you want to do well in school and get into a good college. But I disagree. Stress is toxic. And the scientific research I'll tell you about in a little while completely backs me up. For now, here's a quick summary: Stress changes the structure of your brain, disrupting your concentration, mood, and immune system. Chronic stress not only interferes with memory and learning, it also makes you tired, sick, burned out, and unhappy. Stress can even lead to clinical depression. So rather than motivating you, long-term stress reduces success.

Make no mistake: You don't have to put yourself through torment and heartache to be well-educated and have a good life. Can I promise to eliminate *all* of your stress? If only! The truth is, you'll always have some pressure. There are plenty of things you can't change in high school, such as how much homework you get and who else applies to your first choice college. Stress won't disappear the moment you get accepted to college. It won't end after college, either. No life is problem-free; everyone goes through rough patches. That's why it's such a good idea to learn how to cope as well as possible. As you know, there are no magical solutions. So what, you might be thinking, can you do?

> ### Take a Deep Breath
>
> This quick, easy exercise is scientifically proven to calm you. Take a comfortable seat so your body is well supported and close your eyes. Concentrate on taking deep, full breaths by counting to 4 as you inhale through your nose, then holding your breath for a count of 2, then exhaling slowly to a count of 6. Continue for two to five minutes. Breathe naturally and smoothly (no gasping, please!). As you exhale your stress, notice how your muscles gradually release tension, your limbs growing heavier as they sink restfully into your chair. Then do a scientific test: Ask yourself how you feel now versus before you breathed deeply. The beauty of this exercise is that you can use it anywhere, anytime you want to feel more relaxed.

Well, this I *can* promise you: No matter what level of stress you're feeling now, you can take charge of your life, feel more relaxed, and become happier. It will take time, thought and effort, but you can definitely ease your stress, bit by bit.

Small steps add up to big changes. For example, what if you turned off your bedroom light 15 minutes earlier tonight? Yes, I know, that would mean 15 fewer minutes on Facebook or YouTube….But consider this: Over seven days, you'd be adding at least 105 minutes of peaceful relaxation or nearly two whole hours of sleep you didn't have last week. Sleep, as you'll read later in this book, lets you think more clearly and learn more efficiently, which would actually give you *more* time to be online.

The Plan

This book is going to give you two essential things: (1) **facts** to counteract common misconceptions, set records straight, differentiate truths from myths (for example, about getting into college), and (2) **tools** to use—both right now and over time—that will lower your stress level, restore balance to your life, and help you feel better. I know that these strategies actually work because they've been tested by the teen girls whose honest voices fill these pages. I'm passing their wise suggestions on to you.

The first thing we're going to talk about is where all this toxic stress is coming from. If you're like many girls, you probably feel pulled in too many directions and regret you can never seem to please everyone in your life. We'll explore exactly where your stress is coming from so you can figure out how to get on the path to a calmer, more balanced life.

Next you'll learn why you can't just ignore stress—how it's toxic to your mind and body and prevents you from doing your best. I'll give you specific stress-busting strategies, such as ways to adjust your attitude, take better care of yourself, and figure out which work habits work best for you. Along the way, you'll learn things that may surprise you—for example, that failure is not your enemy and can actually *help* you. No kidding!

You'll also find out more about dealing with stresses such as distracting problems and going through the college process. Lastly, if you're interested, there's an appendix that offers wonderful tips on how to improve your school environment. These come from girls who worked with their teachers and administrators to make changes that would reduce stress for all students.

With a little effort and practice, you'll start to feel lighter and less burdened by stressed. As you feel better, you'll also *do* better. The goal is not perfection. You're aiming to become the best and healthiest version of yourself. Start now by trying this simple exercise.

CHAPTER TWO

Where Stress Comes From

What's causing teen girl stress? As you know, there are many culprits. The demands of academics, extracurricular activities, parents, friends, and technology often cause or worsen stress. Even if you think you already know what's overwhelming you, at least skim these pages for subtle pressures you may not be aware of. When possible, I'll suggest strategies to deal with each of them.

Academics

"I'm a junior and I'm very stressed. The problem is, the homework is endless. I usually don't finish all of it; it's just that I'm too tired to continue. I feel like I'm doing everything I can, but I never catch up. This is the most important year. It's so depressing." —Keisha

"I don't have time for a real weekend anymore. Saturday and Sunday are like myths. They function more like pre-Monday's." —Ruthie

The pressure to get good grades and do well in school is starting very early these days. Even girls who haven't started middle school yet tell me they worry about what scores they'll get on the SATs and where they'll get into school. Little girls should be jumping on trampolines or playing Four Square, not freaking out about college! As you go through middle school and high school, the stress usually worsens. It saddens me to hear girls say parents, teachers, and counselors always remind them, "Everything counts for college." As if you could ever forget!

Here are some basic, stress-minimizing ideas I think every girl should consider:

❋ **Enjoy middle school**. If you're still in middle school, remember that what counts is not every grade, but rather learning to be organized, keeping track of your assignments, and finding effective ways to study. Whatever you do, don't start worrying about high school—and certainly not college.

Bottom line: *Middle school should be a time for making friends, exploring new experiences, and developing skills.*

❋ **Don't think of high school as the "Pre-college Years."** Once you get to high school, don't spend these four years focusing on getting into college. The healthiest goal should be getting to know yourself. When you identify your passions as well as what bores you to death, you'll be more motivated. You'll also know the sorts of colleges where you'll be happiest and most successful.

Bottom line: *High school should be a time of discovering who you are and who you want to be.*

The Case Against AP Classes

If you're taking AP classes to get exempted from college courses, consider this: Many colleges don't accept AP credit, even if you get a good score on the test. And if you intend to major in that subject, you might want to take the intro college class anyway to make sure you have a solid foundation; AP classes are not the same as college-level courses. Also, because high school teachers have to cover everything that's on the AP test, the syllabus is often fixed and less creative, with fewer fun discussions and projects.

❋ **AP & Honors classes are not mandatory**.
You may hear rumors like "colleges want you to take at least 10 AP classes." Well, maybe—or maybe not. It depends on a bunch of things. First, some high schools limit how many AP classes you can take because they go faster and their workload is 40% bigger than non-AP classes. Hmmmmm, you might ask yourself, if I'm already stressed-out, is taking that AP class a great idea? Second, before signing up, decide if you actually like the subject (good reason to take AP) or are just padding your transcript (bad reason to take AP). Third, know that "easy AP class" is an oxymoron; if Statistics doesn't thrill you, imagine having to read 15 pages when you're bleary-eyed at 10 PM.

Bottom line: *Take AP classes only if you love the subject AND have enough time and energy.*

✻ **Take classes that are right for you**. It's easy to get caught up in the hype and compare yourself to "smart" friends who take high-level classes. But it's always best to be where you can succeed. Can you get concepts and keep up with assignments? Do you feel good about contributing to class discussions? Keep in mind: research shows students who feel like "big fish in small ponds" (smarter than their classmates) do better and have higher self-esteem, while those who feel like "small fish in big ponds" (not as capable as their classmates) get poorer grades and feel bad about themselves.

Bottom line: *Be yourself.*

✻ **Keep grades in perspective**. Sure, you want to get good grades, but remember it's not always possible. Maybe you're getting over the flu, super tired, or just having a bad day. So think of a disappointing grade as a chance to learn something—not a cause for a mental breakdown. Ask yourself: Where did I go wrong? Am I missing homework? Not participating enough in class? Learning material superficially? Should I change my study methods—or hit the books sooner?

Bottom line: *Grades signal whether we're doing okay or need to improve.*

✻ **Report cards aren't everything**. The final grades on your report cards aren't the final word on who you are. Your talents may lie in sports, music, drama, art, or people skills, which are hugely important but don't get graded. If you're well-rounded, you may devote tons of time to clubs, student government, or community service.

Bottom line: *You can't expect to do everything—or to do everything extremely well; nobody can.*

Teachers

"All my teachers act as if I only take their class. Or their class is the most important. I'm overloaded with homework, but they are absolutely indifferent and could care less."—Olivia

"Unfair teachers make me extremely stressed, sad, pressured, and depressed when they grade unfairly or give tests on materials we didn't learn."—Lisa

Of course, teachers are human. Some you'll like and connect with more easily than others. Some teaching styles will work for you better than others. My advice? Regardless of how you feel about the people who are teaching you, stay focused on learning. I know that's hard to do. Here are some frequent complaints—and suggestions about what to do about them:

* **"My teacher hates me!"** Though that's possible, it's rather unlikely. Maybe you two got off to a bad start or aren't seeing eye to eye. Or you're not crazy about your teacher and fear you've made your feelings obvious. Maybe you're blaming your teacher because you're struggling in the subject. But DON'T make the mistake of not turning in your assignments. Not only is this a bad way to express anger or frustration, it also won't help a bit. DO be on your best behavior, as if your close friend's parents invited you to dinner. Be on time, look teachers in the eye, listen attentively, smile, and use your best manners. Show them you care by doing your homework and preparing for tests and quizzes. At the end of the day, you may still think they dislike you. But at least you're not giving them reasons to! Plus, getting a bad grade won't spite your teachers; the only one who'll suffer is *you*.

* **"I'm afraid to ask for help."** Some girls are too afraid, embarrassed, or shy to speak up when they have a problem or are confused. Don't be; if you already knew everything, you wouldn't need to be in school. And that's what teachers are there for. Email them to ask questions or get extra help and go over tests after class, during office hours, or when you have a free. Explain why you couldn't do an assignment so your teachers know you're not blowing it off.

* **"The workload in this class is killing me!"** Some teachers are more receptive than others, but if you can be brave and broach the subject, ask for what you need to be successful. If something stressful was going on at home that made it hard for you to finish your homework, you might need an extra day. If your family is going out of town for a vacation, you might ask for an extension on your project so you can do research in the library. Explain these requests politely and matter-of-factly. The worst that can happen is your teacher will say no.

Extracurricular Activities

"Last year my mom kept pushing me to be taking lessons, to be in the school play, and the more she pushed me, the more I wanted her to stop. I'm not rebellious. I get along really well. But she kept drilling it into me, it got to be this big stress, and it made me want to stop even though I love theater."—Ann

"My mom thinks there is ALWAYS a way for me to win/be on top. She pressures me too much when I know I won't win. The other girls are just better at some things."—Natasha

These days, girls feel the need to be spectacular in their extracurricular activities, too. You may not think it's good enough to be in the school band or on the neighborhood soccer team; now you feel pressured to audition for the city youth orchestra or try out for an elite travel team. If by age 3 you haven't taken voice lessons, worked with an acting or voice coach, gotten tutored in Chinese, danced on pointe, or started an instrument, you may think it's too late. Or you may say to yourself, "If I can't be great, why bother?"

This is stress talking. It's harmful because it keeps you from experimenting with new things and having fun—which, as mentioned, should be goals of every girl in middle school and high school.

Here are teen girls' most common extracurricular dilemmas—and ideas about how to resolve them:

- **To play, or not to play?** With schedules already so hectic, many teen girls agonize over whether to continue a sport, club, or music, dance, or community service activity. Hopefully, you aren't basing your decision on whether it'll look good for college. In my opinion, it comes down to this: (1) Do you have the time? and (2) Is it fun? If you answer no to question #2, read no further. If it's not enjoyable, don't do it. Period. When deciding if you have the time, remember to include practices; games, recitals, or tournaments; team dinners; and travel.

- **A great outlet, or another huge pressure?** Has the sport you've loved become just another source of stress? Many girls who play softball or gymnastics, for example, get burned out when tryouts are scarier, competitions become more intense, commitments are more time-consuming, and stakes rise. If pressure outweighs enjoyment, pinpoint the problem. Do you think you have to be the best? If so, adjust your expectations. Maybe just playing the sport and being with teammates is fine. Consider staying on rec teams instead of more competitive travel teams. Or cut back piano lessons to twice a month, forget the recital, and play just for fun. Unless you're hoping to be a professional musician or athlete, reducing the pressure may restore the pleasure.

- **Should you quit?** If there's no compromise—either you do the activity or you don't do it—the decision may be agonizing. Many girls torture themselves because of the years—and loads of parents' money—they've already invested. Do some soul searching. Why do you *really* want to quit? If you've fallen out of love with the activity, take a break and try something else. If you feel guilty about disappointing adults who supported you, remember this should be your call. It's your right to choose your activities; it's your life.

- **Are parents worsening your pressure?** Sometimes girls burn out when their parents care more than they do about games and championships. Do you cringe when you hear parents yelling from the stands? This has become a huge problem in our culture. *Mary*, a competitive swimmer, says, *"When I don't improve my time in a race, my mother goes all silent in the car ride home. I feel like such a disappointment."* If that's true for you, it's time for a heart-to-heart with your parents. If that seems hard, ask a coach or trusted relative to help.

- **Are you "bad" or even "the worst" at your activity?** Okay, even if you really are, so what? Remember, you don't have to be great at everything. In fact, you can still be a great person and not be great at *anything*. If you completely suck at lacrosse or look like a duck trying to pirouette, big deal. Don't take it so seriously. Better yet, if you can laugh at yourself you'd probably have even more fun. Besides, this could be a humorous anecdote to include in your memoirs one day...

Parents

"As soon as I get home from school, my mother starts in on me. It's all she cares about anymore. She's always going, 'Let me check your work. This answer could be better. Did you make those note cards I suggested yet? Let me see your thesis statement for your English paper; it's due on Friday.' She's always on my case. For God's sake, I'm not in third grade anymore!"—Morgan

"My parents keep pressuring me to get better grades. I'm really trying, but nothing is good enough for them. All they care about is getting into college. I really love them and want to make them happy, but I don't think I have the potential to do what they want me to do."—Perri

Your parents love you and want you to be healthy and happy. But they may not always be attuned to your pressures—or that they're making them worse. Can you have a chat with the parentals? Using a calm and respectful voice, tell them honestly how you feel and what they can do to help. Try role playing first with a teacher, guidance counselor, older sibling, or relative. There's no guarantee your parents will get it or make the changes you want. But it pays to speak up and give them a chance. Girls say these situations most often worsen their stress:

- **Parents' expectations are overly specific or unrealistic**. My research was clear: stress is worse when parents expect certain grades, prizes, and college stickers on the family car. If you can admit to mom and/or dad, "I'd like to make you proud, but I don't know if I can," you may spark a helpful conversation. Parents sometimes forget not to compare siblings, who usually have different strengths, interests, and opportunities. Also, I often remind them that some goals require time and patience. Because the teen brain develops through the mid-twenties, classes that are challenging or even impossible for you now may be a piece of cake in a year or two.

- **Micromanagement**. If your parents constantly monitor tests and assignments, you may be annoyed enough to rebel. How? By doing the opposite of what they want. In other words, the more they push or nag, the less you do. Suggest that if they trust you, they might back off. Ask what will convince them they don't need to be as involved. Assure mom and dad you'll ask for help when you need it—and make good on that promise.

- **Unhelpful (aka stress-inducing) questions**. The minute you walk in the door after school, do you hear, "What do you have to do tonight?" or "What did you get on your science test? What was the class average?" These well-intentioned but irksome questions often provoke snarky comments and meltdowns. Then parents wonder, "What did I say?" Ask mom or dad to give you a few minutes to chill when you get home. Explain that you have to think about your day before you can talk about it. Ask that dinner conversations be neutral and stress-free—for example, by talking about topics other than school.

- **Parental advice is outdated**. Some advice you get is helpful, while others…not so much. That's probably because it's based on their experiences at your age. Guidance counselors can be awfully handy here. Ask your parents to chat with your advisor or college counselor. Also, share with them my chapter on truths and myths about college.

- **Parental "consequences" are harsh**. To help teens do better in school, some parents take away distractions such as TV, cell phones, and computers. To you, this "help" may be cruel and unusual punishment. It may make you angry or resentful. It's true that screens are huge temptations, highly addictive, and the #1 cause of girls' procrastination. But I believe an important goal during middle school and high school should be learning how to manage technology. Work with your parents to negotiate reasonable guidelines—and stick to them.

Friends—Social Stress

"I'm scared that my current friends are going to hurt me because my past friends have."—Rory

"It's stressful to deal with fake people. Girls can be mean."—Annaliese

"Boys are really stressful. Are you going to ask me to Homecoming, or not? Quit with the mixed messages!"—Ginger

"My friends are all really, really smart. They're in honors and AP classes and get nothing below an A. I try not to compare myself to them, but I'm in regular classes, and it's sometimes hard for me just to get B's."—Claire

Social lives can be stressful—in so many ways. How could they not be? Besides dealing with heaps of homework, nagging parents, and demanding coaches, you may have all sorts of stuff going on with your friends that stresses you out. Here are the top 5 issues I hear about:

- **Trying to fit in and be popular**. Most girls want to feel accepted and have friends to hang out with in school. Otherwise, you may feel awkward in class, lonely in the cafeteria, and too self-conscious to participate in class. Do you worry about seeming too smart, or not smart enough? *Aimee*, says, *"The girls at my school judge me because I look different. I don't wear what everybody else wears. If I say anything in class, they all stare. I'm not good in sports. Gym is a nightmare."* Aimee spends way more energy worrying about what kids at school think—and finding excuses to hide in the nurse's office—than her schoolwork.

- **Competing with friends—over everything**. Whether it's grades, SAT scores, athletic tryouts, or play auditions, girls who constantly compare themselves to others are more stressed-out. Two classic scenarios: You're feeling okay about your 88 on an English paper—until your friend has a meltdown over her 92. Or, you aced a test in a subject she's struggling in—but when she asks what you got you don't want to make her feel bad. Nothing good usually comes from comparing grades. So why not adopt a "let's not talk about it" policy? If a classmate or friend asks, try casually saying, "Let's not go there!" "I did okay," "It stresses me out more to talk about grades," or whatever feels most comfortable and natural to you.

- **Making social plans is distracting**. *Maya* described it well: *"It's distracting when you're trying to figure out your plans on the weekend. It's hard to sit down and do work on a Saturday when you're stressed out about what to do that night or when you're waiting for your friends to decide stuff and get back to you."* Feeling like you're being excluded or left out of plans is even more painful. This happens to everyone at times, but if it becomes a pattern consider whether your friends are loyal and reliable enough—or if making new ones should be on your to-do list.

- **Dramas consume time and emotional energy**. Social dramas are pretty high up on most girls' stress list. It's hard work to maintain friendships and navigate cliques in school. Although every relationship has its ups and downs, the downs make stress worse. As *Terry* says, *"My mind wanders, especially if I'm in a fight with someone. I can't stop thinking about it and I can't concentrate."* It's also stressful when girls in your friendship group are having issues with each other. If it's too much, distance yourself by hanging out with other people. Truly mean people are toxic; protect yourself from the hurt and the drama.

- **Friends' problems are stressful**. It's also stressful when friends you really care about go through hard times. Besides worrying about them, you might spend tons of time talking to them or discussing how to help them with other people. In these cases, be just as kind to yourself as to your friend. For example, don't make things worse for yourself by cutting class or ignoring your work. Rather than taking this on alone, get support by enlisting adults who are trained to help, such as teachers, guidance counselors, school social workers, and psychologists.

The Media

"You have the media with all those super skinny girls with perfect hair and make-up and clothes. It's terrible. We can't keep up."—Hannah

If you read magazines, watch TV, or go to the movies, you're bombarded with images of ideal, sexy girls with flawless skin and hair, dressed in great clothes, usually posed with hot guys who can't take their eyes off them. Um, who wouldn't feel inadequate? But if you're even tempted to compare yourself, remember what you're seeing isn't real life. It's a photo shoot. Models don't stumble out of bed looking gorgeous. In fact, they have zits and bad hair days. But then they sit in chairs for hours and hours while teams of hair, makeup, and wardrobe people work on them. Even after all that, their photos are airbrushed. So much for perfection!

Technology

"I have found myself becoming very self-conscious about how I look on the internet. I'm obsessed with it and it adds to my stress."—Lainie

"You want to look cool on Facebook. You want people to know that you have a lot of friends and do interesting things."—Nina

Who doesn't love their cell phone, laptop, MP3 player, and game console? Truly, it's hard to imagine being without all this technology. But we also can't ignore the fact that these screens are adding more and more to every teen girl's stress level:

- **Procrastination**. This has become the number one problem for busy teen girls, which is so major I'm going to talk about it more later on.

- **Creating profiles**. *Cara* put this well when she said, *"Facebook is giving you another way of comparing yourself. It's adding to the pressure to be somebody else, somebody idealized and perfect. You can't see anyone's flaws; they're all filtered out."* Trying to portray yourself a certain way online not only takes up a lot of time and mental energy, but also adds to your self-consciousness and anxiety.

- **The stress of not being yourself**. The desire for people to see you a certain way can create a gap between how you portray yourself and who you really are. *Chelsea* says, *"On Facebook you write down books you've never read. You say Anna Karenina is your favorite book, but really it's Gossip Girl."* Being someone you're not wastes too much energy. Besides, being genuine is much cooler.

- **Insecurity about popularity**. Do you measure how popular you are by how many friends you have on Facebook, how many people *like* your photos or posts, or the number of texts you get? Rather than getting caught up in this competition, ask yourself which is more meaningful and makes you happier: hanging out with fun, amazing, trusted friends, or tallying up the number of random people you interact with online.

- **Never unplugged**. Since cell phones are almost always on, most people are constantly waiting for the next incoming message. This causes a rush of pleasure when the brain releases dopamine, the feel-good chemical. It's so addicting! But always being on hyper-alert, waiting for the next buzz or signal that someone's thinking of you, is stressful. When you're not supposed to be checking your phone, it's even more stressful to try to control your curiosity and resist peeking. And when your phone goes silent and your dopamine level drops, you can get bummed, out of sorts, or anxious.

- **Pressure to answer immediately**. Because texting is nearly instantaneous, it's natural to expect friends to respond right away. Many girls tell me that when they don't, they worry: Are friends ignoring them? Angry at them? Same goes for when you get a text and can't answer immediately. Do you worry your friends will get ticked off at you? Not being in constant contact can be stressful.

- **Texts are hard to interpret**. Because text messages don't give you nonverbal cues like tone of voice, inflection, facial expression, and body language, it's tricky to interpret their exact meaning. When you read, "Good for you!" for example, you might be confused. Was your friend sincerely complimenting you? Being sarcastic? Teasing? The intention is totally unclear. Taking texts the wrong way can lead to major cyberdramas.

- **Increased social paranoia**. Thanks to photos posted on Facebook, you know when your friends were out somewhere with each other—but without you. It's easy to wonder, "Why wasn't I invited?" *Dana* says, *"When you get mobile uploads you realize everybody else is out having fun except for you. You're the only loser."*

- **The danger of sexts**. Some girls send suggestive, sexy, or naked photos of themselves, only to be utterly humiliated when so-called friends or ex-boyfriends forward them to the entire school. Many end up so miserable it's hard to return to their schools. Hopefully this hasn't happened to you or your friends. To avoid the unbearable stress this can cause, there's a very simple solution: Just don't sext.

CHAPTER THREE

How Stress Kills Success

"Nothing is good enough, no matter how hard I try."—Gladys

"I'm a junior and my stress story starts around 5th or 6th grade. The stress, exhaustion, and habits have built up with nowhere to go. I've gotten to the point where I honestly do not care anymore."—Sammi

Because stress has become such a huge problem, it's good that people are starting to realize how harmful it can be—and beginning to suggest ways to combat it. Recently, an article called, "Is the Life You're Living Worth the Price You're Paying to Live It?" appeared in a highly respected journal, the Harvard Business Review. Although it was geared for business professionals, I think this is the exact question every teen girl should ask herself. To answer it, you first have to know the toll chronic stress is taking on you, your mind, and your body.

What's so bad about cheating yourself of a little sleep, skipping breakfast or grabbing something unhealthy, trying to pay attention in seven or eight classes, doing your best on tests or papers, pushing through when your eyes keep closing after lunch (that is, if you've eaten at all), dragging yourself to after school activities and athletic practices or games, heading home to piles of homework and tests to study for the next day, and then falling into bed at midnight worrying about either forgetting to do something or not doing something well enough?

This hectic, pressure-filled life floods your body with stress hormones (for example, adrenalin and cortisol, in case you're wondering) that are designed to give you instant energy to survive threatening, life-or-death situations. In the short run, this system works great. When predators endangered our ancestors, stress hormones revved up their heart rate and blood pressure, pumping oxygen to their muscles so they could fight, flee, or freeze—the three biological responses to threats. These days, bodies still behave the same way, but pressure-filled modern lifestyles are causing more constant stress—and therefore physical, mental, and emotional damage. Here's how stress may be killing your success:

Depression

Stress that's mild and brief actually feels *good*. That's because stress-induced cortisol stimulates the brain to release dopamine, a hormone associated with pleasure. A rush of dopamine makes us feel great: we're highly alert, our senses are fully alive, and our thinking is sharp. In other words, we feel *stimulated*. The weird thing is, you may really enjoy—and even pay for—certain kinds of brief, mildly stressful experiences. Two examples? Scary movies and roller coaster rides.

But the operative words here are *mild* and *brief*. Imagine how you would feel if a roller coaster ride were two hours long or a terrifying movie lasted all day. It would stop being fun, for sure. You also wouldn't be thrilled if the stress became severe—say, if your leg got twisted painfully in the roller coaster. That's because moderate or chronic stress has the exact opposite effect in the brain—and therefore on your mood and well-being. Long-term stress depletes the brain of dopamine, so you start feeling awful. You're tired, down in the dumps, and apathetic. Nothing seems fun anymore. As you may have realized, the end result of chronic stress that I'm describing is *depression*.

Deteriorating Thinking

When you're anxious, fearful, or stressed-out, one part of your brain starts firing like mad. This basically shuts down another area of your brain, the one that lets you think logically and use good judgment. So when you're stressed-out, you become reactive and impulsive rather than reflective and thoughtful. Think about the last time something made you so furious that before you knew it you had flipped out. You didn't even get to think about the consequences of what you were doing—such as the trouble you were landing yourself in. Chronic stress does the same thing: your thinking brain essentially goes into hibernation mode.

To accurately size up situations and make smart decisions, you have to stay cool. That requires calming your emotions and quieting your mind. You'll soon be learning better ways to care of your body, mind, and spirit. But for now, remember that breathing deeply even for one minute can completely clear your body of the toxic effects of the stress hormone cortisol. So here's a wise strategy: take 60 seconds before starting a test or class presentation just to breathe deeply.

Demoralizing You—and Your Performance

If you're motivated to do well and achieve your goals (you are or you wouldn't be reading this book), you should know that nonstop stress will eventually ruin your performance, kill your motivation, and demoralize you. Bessie is a good example. Although she's usually confident about her speaking skills and was well-prepared for a recent presentation, she froze. Why? Right before she started, she thought about how much she wanted to impress her English teacher, do better than the superstar classmate who went right before her, and avoid getting a bad grade that would anger her parents.

As you now know, putting that kind of incredible pressure on herself caused a jolt of stress hormones to shut down Bessie's thinking brain. Shaking with fear and panic, how could she possibly stand up in front of the class and give her best presentation?

Stress also affects the brain structure you use in creating new memories—that is, when learning. With chronic stress, your brain learns much less effectively, so it's harder to remember French vocabulary words, what led up to World War II, or how eye color is determined genetically. Ever wonder why you did badly on a test even though you studied? Stress may have prevented you from learning the material well—plus, your mind might have gone blank during the test.

Who wouldn't get upset and frustrated? It seems so unfair. Then, the worse you do, the more hopeless you feel about ever doing well. Over time, you can start thinking of *yourself* as hopeless, and that's when you may stop trying. Maybe you'll convince yourself it's because you don't care anymore—even though, deep down, you do care. It's human nature to protect yourself from painful thoughts. As *Dana* put it, *"If I try and don't do well, I must be stupid. I blow off school because I'd rather be bad than dumb."*

Sleep Deprivation

Whether you cheat yourself of zzzzz's because you have too much to do or can't fall asleep because your brain won't turn off, sleep deprivation causes a boatload of problems. One, without enough sleep your brain can't strengthen memories well, so you'll perform worse on tests. Two, while you might do okay with simple memorization, sleep deprivation messes up higher-level thinking such as critical analysis, understanding abstract concepts, and appreciating how ideas relate to each another.

Three, our immune systems need rest to keep us healthy. When you're stressed-out and run down, you get sick more often. Then you're absent more, work piles up, you get more stressed, and you stay up even later to get it all done. What a mess!

Not Enough Downtime

Are you so busy that you have hardly any downtime? (I hope you're not wondering, "What's downtime?") You know, when you do things just for fun, just for you, or do "nothing." You lie on your bed, stare into space, daydream, or let your mind wander. Although parents often think of this time as "unproductive," it can be absolutely invaluable. You get to review conversations (e.g., with your crush or boyfriend), process experiences, and discover things about yourself or other people. Also, spending time by yourself fosters creativity. So stop worrying about your college apps and use downtime to draw, compose music, write poetry, journal, or just muse.

Vulnerability to Serious Problems

If you're so focused on external signs of success (e.g., grades, scores, team wins, and awards), you can easily lose touch with what's even more important: your *inner* life. This includes your thoughts and feelings as well as realizations about what intrigues you, what you're passionate about, and whether you need to make changes.

If you go through the motions just to get through the day, you lose touch with your inner life and become a stranger to yourself. This is really unhealthy. Some girls begin to feel as if their outward persona, the one they show to others, is not their true self. Being estranged from your authentic self can lead to depression, eating disorders, or risky and self-harming behaviors like cutting.

Coping Unhealthily

When you're overwhelmed, you can feel desperate to make yourself feel better. If you don't learn healthy strategies to manage stress, you might resort to potentially harmful ways. Be brutally honest with yourself as you consider whether you're:

- ❖ ***Craving stimulants***. Are you drinking tons of caffeinated beverages or binging on chocolate, sugar, or junk food? Although the occasional splurge is fine, if you're using them regularly it'll be even harder to fall asleep at night. Plus, chocolate and sugar are great comfort foods, but not especially nutritious as brain fuel.

- ❖ ***Using Substances***. Years ago, fewer teen girls than boys started to use weed, tobacco, and alcohol. But this trend is reversing. Girls, this is one race you don't want to win! Also, many people are using tranquilizers, barbiturates, and sedatives from home medicine cabinets—not to get a buzz, but rather to escape from stress, gain confidence, improve mood, and cope better with problems. Substances are *not* the answer; they cause far more problems than they solve.

- ❖ ***Smoking Cigarettes***. Most adults think peer pressure causes teens to start smoking cigarettes. But only 15% of girls say that's why they first light up. The same number say they want to experiment, be thin, or look cool. Why do a whopping 70% of girls (but only 56% of boys) turn to cigs? No surprise: to relieve stress! Even worse, due to teen girls' brain chemistry, you can become hooked on tobacco after only a few cigarettes. That's exactly what the tobacco industry wants, of course, as they entice you with sexy ads. But besides exposing you to toxins that cause cancer, smoking makes you age faster. Nicotine discolors and wrinkles your skin. It's a nasty and expensive habit.

- ❖ ***Using Alcohol.*** In case you missed these facts in Health, here's what every teen girl should know:

    - ❖ The teen brain can't metabolize alcohol as well as the adult brain

    - ❖ Drinking impairs memory and learning by damaging the part of the brain responsible for them

    - ❖ Starting to drink before age 15 makes you four times likelier to develop a drinking problem

    - ❖ Getting drunk is associated with greater—and less wise—sexual activity, which often leads to poor self-esteem and depression

Cheating

Another way of coping with intense academic pressure is cheating. But you already know that. Studies confirm that high school students are using every angle and advantage they can to get ahead, regardless of whether they know it's wrong. A psychologist studying this issue for more than 25 years recently found that 90% of high school students reported cheating in one way or another—whether plagiarizing, copying other people's work, buying papers, taking stuff from the Internet, or even hiring brainy classmates to take SATs for them.

It's easy to justify boosting your own GPA when you think, "everybody else cheats." And mostly everybody gets away with it. But when your inner voice tells you something is wrong, pay close attention or you won't feel good about yourself. Plus, research shows that the honesty and integrity you develop in school are habits that determine how you act later in life. Recently, a slew of Harvard undergrads were expelled in a huge cheating scandal. After graduation, too, students who have cheated in school are dishonest in their business practices. Decide not to go down this particular road. You're much better off hitting the books and keeping your eyes on your own tests.

You still might be stressed out by friends or classmates asking to cheat off you (e.g., "Can I copy your math homework?" or "I'm taking a make-up science test next period; what were the essay questions?"). *Geri* says, *"I want to help my friend, but it's wrong. I don't want to say no, but I don't want to agree either."* Keep in mind that even if it everyone else seems to be cheating, you don't have to. If you want to help a friend, offer to go over her homework, explain a tricky math problem, or study with her instead.

Burnout

Remember the fun of elementary school: illustrating book reports, doing cool projects, and writing creative stories? Maybe you enjoyed learning about U.S. Presidents, the animal kingdom, or customs of Native American tribes. But if your four years of high school are filled with sky-high stress, you can kiss your love of learning goodbye. Remember that knowledge expands your appreciation for life, satisfies your curiosity, and suggests exciting new ideas and places to explore. Don't let the hype about achievement or pressures to get into the "right" college kill that enthusiasm.

Speaking of life after high school, I see many girls who think, "All I have to do is get into college and all the stress will be over." Sorry, but that's not true. According to the Higher Educational Research Institute at UCLA, which has been tracking this for 25 years, freshmen are arriving at college in worse psychological shape than ever before. As usual, girls are even more overwhelmed than boys by everything they have to do—and that gap is widening every year. So if you're hoping all your stress will magically disappear after high school, think again. You have to start working on this *now*.

There is lots more you can do to get rid of or at least minimize pressure. I promise! The rest of the book is devoted to just that. Next, we're going to talk about a huge part of stress: Attitude. Fortunately, this is one area where you have plenty of control. You'll learn many different ways to adjust your outlook that will calm and focus your mind to boost your performance and better reach your goals.

CHAPTER FOUR

Failure is Your Friend
(& Other Attitude Adjustments)

"I feel nothing but pressure in school. Teachers and parents have such high expectations that it is hard to live up to. But the person I feel most pressure from is myself. If I don't do well, I get upset and depressed."—Taylor

"I'm a perfectionist and I worry a lot about everything, especially what others think. How do I stop thinking so much about that?"—Jessica

"For me, stress is all about the little things—small things I've done wrong that I know shouldn't bother me but still do. I focus and dwell on them, and they pile up until I feel like I've just been doing everything wrong in life."—Cici

So far we've discussed how parents, teachers, coaches, friends, siblings, technology, advertising and the media all contribute to teen girl stress. But who's usually the worst culprit? As Taylor describes, it's you! You're terribly demanding of yourself. Sure, being motivated and hard-working pays off. But the added stress isn't necessary—and, as you've learned, is actually harming you and your success.

On top of that, many of you are perfectionists who set the bar extremely high, perhaps unrealistically, expect excellence at all times, and beat yourselves up whenever you fall short. But this mindset is self-defeating. Anxious, rigid thoughts actually hold you back. If this sounds like you, attitude adjustments are in order!

Stop Catastrophizing!

"School is very important to me. I always do all of my work. If I don't get an A on everything, I start to cry and think that the world is over."—Renee

Many stressed-out girls see every paper or test as the final word on whether they'll be successful. With the stakes that high, no wonder anxiety runs amok. What pops into your mind as you sit down to an exam? Do you think "If I don't ace this test, _____ will happen"? Fill in the blank with: "my GPA will be ruined," "my parents will kill me," "I'll never get into my #1 college," or other worst-case scenarios. Do you obsess that: a C+ in chemistry will keep you out of honors science next year? A falling out with your best friend will permanently exile you from your group? Or being dumped means no one so cute will ever ask you out again?

It's important to catch yourself when your thoughts go from small mistakes, setbacks, or disappointments to out-and-out tragedies. Dire predictions are really just thoughts distorted by fear. Things are rarely as bad as you may think. Even awful times don't last forever. To stop your negative or catastrophic thinking, try a technique a girl I know uses all the time. *Deena says, "Focus on where you are right now, what you're supposed to be doing, and what's happening in the present. That way, you can't be worrying about the future."* Great idea! Try it.

To make yourself feel better, also try: (a) distracting yourself with a silly sitcom, (b) thinking of how to handle similar situations better in the future, and (c) using tried-and-true comforts such as a bubble bath, a talk with a special friend, a run with your dog, or a warm chocolate chip cookie.

Accept What You Can't Control

No matter how hard you work, sometimes a little bad luck gets in your way. Despite preparing brilliantly for your audition, for example, you might wake up that morning with a sore throat or because of blatant favoritism that part may go to someone else. Yes, it is outrageously unfair, but that's life. There are times when for no good reason you won't achieve a goal you've been striving for. There's nothing you can do except accept it and move on.

This may sound corny, but disappointments can turn out to be truly amazing opportunities. You might not notice that at first because you're so upset. But with time, you can start to get some perspective and see things differently. Maybe when you don't get that part you wanted in the school play, you decide to help direct—and soon realize *that's* your real calling. As the saying goes, "when one door closes, another door opens." So when you get over frustration or dashed hopes, discover what new possibilities may be available. Be flexible and think out of the box.

Why Failure is Your Friend—Really!

Of course, nobody *wants* to fall short. It's normal to feel sad, frustrated, discouraged, embarrassed, and a whole host of other emotions after letdowns. But there are two enormously important things to know about failure:

(1) **To truly succeed, you have to be willing to risk failure**. If you don't fall flat on your face every now and then, it means you're not setting your sights high enough. You're too cautious, staying within your comfort zone and sticking to what you know. If you're afraid to take Mandarin because it's supposedly hard to learn and go for Spanish, which you speak at home, you'll ace your foreign language final but never experience the satisfaction of conquering a challenging goal or realize your dream of being an exchange student in China.

(2) **What defines you are not your successes, but how you handle failures**. When you encounter a personal setback, do you deny it? Blame other people? Hide under the covers in shame? Say, 'Forget it. I'm never trying that again'? Or do you figuratively get up, dust yourself off, and decide what to do differently next time?

When he spoke at a conference not long ago, *Biz Stone, the* co-founder of Twitter, said that *"Failure looks good on your resume because then people know you're actually human."* These days, failure may actually be your ticket to internships, jobs, or graduate school. That's because interviewers will probably ask you what you learned from them. Your answer will speak volumes to potential employers about who you are, your attitude, determination, and character. *Bill Gates*, chairman of Microsoft, has said, *"It's fine to celebrate success, but it is more important to heed the lessons of failure."* So think of yours as potential goldmines.

Dealing with failure also creates flexibility and resiliency—two extremely important skills. Getting benched in soccer, rejected from National Honor Society, or dumped by a crush help you learn to cope with life's inevitable letdowns. Small doses of disappointment and frustration inoculate you against getting overwhelmed by bigger disasters. *Beverly Cleary*, the beloved author of many children's books, described in her memoir that after getting a D in a college science course, she lugged around her huge science textbook so she could study many times a day. She got an A for the semester, her D was erased, and she earned a B+ for the year. More important, she wrote, *"I had learned a lesson more valuable than botany."*

Challenge Your Assumptions

Are you living in the shadow of a highly successful brother or sister? Girls often stress themselves out by thinking that being *different* from superstar siblings means they're *inferior*. If your older sister was Miss Popularity, you might feel like a social outcast if you have only a couple of close friends. Or, the reverse could be true; if your sister stayed in every weekend to do homework and practice her violin, you might fear being a slacker or party girl if you value going out and socializing with friends.

Comparing yourself to sibs who are natural athletes can freak you out, too. If, say, your brother is a varsity athlete who wins all sorts of awards, you may think it's dumb to go out for a team if you can't be that good. But challenge that assumption. So what if you aren't? Maybe you're a terrific team player who glues the team together and raises spirit. Your parents should be just as proud of these qualities (and may secretly wish your brother had more of them, as well).

There's Always Someone Better

As great as you are, you can't always be the best. The truth is, there will always be people who are smarter, cuter, more athletic, taller, sexier, more creative, or more ambitious than you are. That's true for absolutely everyone. But it's okay; who ever said you have to be the best? In fact, it's a waste of valuable time, attention, and energy to compare yourself to other people. It would be a shame to avoid activities or classes that interest you just because you fear you won't shine. Lose the attitude and go for it!

The truth is, it's much harder for girls when parents don't honor and support each child's individuality. In some families, every kid is expected to be exactly the same, as if they were formed with a cookie cutter. Since Miranda's parents and older brother went to a rigorous independent school in their town, they expected her to go there, too. She felt as if that script had been written for her the day she was born. Because she struggled with learning issues, it was hard for her to feel comfortable and excel at that school. It wasn't a good fit for Miranda.

Even if your parents won't budge from their hard-and-fast ideas about what your success should look like, give yourself permission to figure out your true passions and what works best for you. Surround yourself with supportive adults such as advisors and counselors. Consider the great advice of *Steve Jobs*, co-founder and former CEO of Apple, who once said, *"Your time is limited, so don't waste it living someone else's life. Don't let the noise of other's opinions drown out your own inner voice."*

Be Your Own Champion

Whatever you do, don't give up on yourself, even if adults in your life have definite opinions about what your success should look like, are overly invested in your wins and losses, or expect too much. The worst thing you can do is quit your sport or give up in school. That's just hurting you and sabotaging your dreams. Plus, spiting parents is just another way of giving them control. Being truly independent means being yourself and listening to your authentic inner voice, no matter what anyone else thinks.

Practice Shouldn't Make Perfect

While an undergrad at Smith College, Melissa Fares wisely argues in her writing against the motto "practice makes perfect." Since perfection is unattainable, she suggests the real goal of practice should be improvement.

Avoid Perfection at all Costs

It's wonderful to be ambitious, conscientious, and hardworking. It's great to be organized, efficient, and competent, as well as to persevere until you reach your goals. You may also try to be polite, cheerful, and helpful. Perhaps you want to be a good student, friend, sister, girlfriend, and daughter. On top of that you may want to look fabulous and stay thin.

This is all fine and good unless you drive yourself mercilessly to achieve ALL this—and at all times. In other words, if you think you have to be perfect. Because being a perfectionist is a surefire recipe for creating horrific levels of stress. In fact, psychologists associate perfectionism with anxiety, depression, eating disorders, and self-destructive behaviors.

You might be wondering: What's the difference between being motivated to do really great in school and activities—and a perfectionist who's at risk for all these serious problems? Let's compare two girls who both have tons of friends and do equally well grade-wise:

Bianca sets super high goals for herself and can't stand not meeting them. She says, *"The most important thing is being right. I feel like I need to be correct in whatever situation I'm in. I know it's unrealistic, but I strive hard. I can't mess up."* Bianca twists herself into a pretzel to avoid making mistakes. She often stays up until all hours. No achievement makes her truly happy. If she gets an A, she worries that she won't do as well on the next test. She always has to prove herself. Bianca used to love school, but now she dreads Mondays, often gets migraines, and feels exhausted all the time.

Mara loves to read and learn new things. After watching a little TV after school, she tackles her homework. She studies a lot for tests and is generally confident about doing well. If she doesn't get a good grade, she sees her teacher to find out where she went wrong. Mara enjoys challenges; she signed up for AP Calculus even though she knows it'll be hard for her to do well. She likes getting feedback from her teachers. Mara sees herself as a top student, but it's her wit, sense of justice, and ability to get along with all kinds of different people that make her feel good about herself.

See the difference? It's all in the attitude. Accept that you're not perfect. There is no such thing as the perfect teen girl, the perfect college, the perfect friend, or the perfect job. It's okay to be frustrated, to not always be super friendly, and even to complain or vent sometimes. That makes you refreshingly human. Ironically, the quicker you accept your shortcomings—and, even better, to find the humor in them—the easier it will be for you to be the best possible you.

Karla, a high school student I interviewed while traveling, tripped as she sat down one morning, laughed out loud, and announced dramatically, *"And ... for my grand entrance!"* A teacher told me about another buoyant girl: *"Leann is a hopeless athlete, but she thinks it's hilarious. She can make mistakes and not be good at something. That makes her so much stronger than girls who can't do that."*

Similarly, we can all learn from *Kiera*, a resilient Girls' Life reader, who can be compassionate toward herself: *"Nobody is perfect. We are all human beings who make mistakes. We all get a bad grade every now and then, but you build off of it. You fix your mistakes. The purpose of school is to learn. I try to be the best that I can possibly be, and my best is enough."*

Keep Things in Perspective

This may be hard to remember, especially when you're in the thick of midterms, projects are due, you've got to sign up for the SATs before the deadline, and you have double practices for field hockey, but high school isn't your entire life. It's only four years. You don't have to reach all your goals during this time. Seriously, that's an understatement. There's plenty of time to discover things about yourself and develop skills when you're in college or beyond. This isn't a race.

Another thing to keep in mind is that there's more to life than academics. School is only a small part of it. Recently, one of the students at a school I visited in Dallas expressed this well. *"Yes, I'm working hard,"* she said. *"In some classes that's an A; in some it's a B or C. In the end, people won't remember my GPA or whether I went to an Ivy. They'll remember how I made them feel. My faith and relationships are more important in the long run."*

CHAPTER FIVE

Taking Care of You

"I take a 30-minute break in between school and homework by sleeping, reading, or watching TV."—Zoe

You probably hear no shortage of advice on how to reduce stress. The trouble is, some of these suggestions may seem ridiculous, unrealistic, or contradictory, which can stress you out even more. In this chapter, you'll hear about strategies teen girls say *really* work for them, along with scientific facts to back them up. Remember, nothing is guaranteed to work for everyone. To find which are best for you, try them. Sadly, no technique will make your stress completely disappear. But you're not going to feel any better if you do *nothing*. In fact, the stress may even get worse. So make a little effort, even for five to ten minutes every day. Just one stress-busting strategy can make a huge difference.

The first step is thinking about how to create a healthy balance of work, play, and rest in your life. That's key. If you want to perform at your best, you've got to take care of yourself. I know, I know, with your schedule and all the things on your To Do list, it's easier said than done. But here are pretty basic ideas for nurturing your body, mind, and spirit that don't eat up a lot of time.

Your Body

Rest and Relax

- **Sleep**. Ideally, teens are supposed to get 8 to 10 hours of sleep every night. Yeah, right! Only a few girls are fortunate to be that well-rested. But as you learned earlier, you can't afford to cheat yourself of sleep if you want a healthy body and well-functioning brain. Decide on the minimum number of hours you will sleep, no matter what's due the next day. Before bed, avoid "blue" screens like TVs, cell phones, and computers, which signal your brain to stay awake. Try spraying your pillow with lavender. Find a sleep-inducing ritual that relaxes your body and mind before turning in at night.

- **Maintain a schedule**. Sleep researchers say keeping to the same schedule every day gets your body in a rhythm. The truth is, though, many teens crave sleeping in on the weekends to catch up on zzzzs lost during the school week. It's bliss to turn off your alarm and know you can lounge in your comfy bed on Saturdays and Sundays. But know that if you sleep until 1 in the afternoon, it'll be harder to fall asleep at a reasonable hour Sunday night—and to wake up without a struggle Monday morning.

- **Take frequent breaks**. During marathon homework or study sessions, especially during crunch times like midterms and finals, make sure you rest often. Schedule a break either every 45 or 60 minutes, after finishing assignments, or as you cross off smaller tasks. And, um, no hour-long breaks, please…plan for 10 or 15 minutes, and then set your alarm to remind you in case you forget.

- **Power naps**. Nothing beats a little afternoon siesta to rejuvenate energy and boost mental power. Plus, by lowering cortisol—that nasty stress hormone we keep talking about—napping strengthens the immune system and therefore helps you to stay healthy. Again, set your phone alarm for 20 to 30 minutes. A 90-minute deep sleep is likely to leave you groggy and disoriented rather than refreshed.

- **Relaxation techniques**. Besides learning techniques to relax your body, such as deep muscle relaxation, which is described in the box below, try a sauna, steam bath, whirlpool, bubble bath, hot shower, or massage.

Movement

"Recently, I've started exercising, and after a 30 minute to an hour run/walk outdoors I feel happy and healthy."—Kelsey

"I go to the gym. When I get home I don't feel tired, I just feel like all the anger is gone and I am more productive and not so likely to snap."—Violet

Aside from sleep, scientists say exercise is best thing for blowing off steam and relieving stress. Plus, the exercise releases endorphins, those brain chemicals we talked about earlier that produce a natural high. To feel good and perform at your best, you have to get up and move. Ideally, you should alternate between movement and relaxation. According to researchers in Amsterdam, kids who get more exercise do better in school. They get higher grades and better scores on math, language, and general thinking and memory tests. Scientists are unsure whether movement improves concentration or if it increases blood flow to the brain. But they know it works.

That's why researchers recommend a minimum of 15 to 20 minutes of vigorous physical activity (preferably outdoors) at least three times per week. New studies say you get the same benefit from exercising just 10 minutes or less a few times during the day rather than all at once. This is easier to do. When you're taking breaks from studying or doing your homework at home, whenever possible go outside. Take a brisk walk to mail a letter, do an errand, or walk your dog.

Deep Muscle Relaxation

• • •

Basic instructions: Sit comfortably in a chair or lay on the floor. Working on one area of your body at a time, contract your muscles for a count of three, and then relax them. Concentrate on feeling tension drain from your body. Start with your head. Squeeze your eyes tightly shut, then release. Scrunch your forehead, then release. Press your lips tightly together. Open your mouth as widely as possible. Feel your facial muscles relax. Move on to your neck. Touch your chin to your chest. Then raise your chin and let your head fall back. Next, raise your shoulders to your ears. Then lower them. Necks and shoulders are notorious holders of stress, so do this again if it feels good. Tighten your fists. Curl your biceps. Pull your stomach muscles in. Then push your abdominal muscles out as far as they will go. Tighten your glutes (the butt), followed by your thigh muscles and calves. Point your toes. Then flex your feet. Notice how relaxed each of your muscles feel after the tension releases. Do this exercise first thing in the morning to start off your day calmly and last thing at night for deeper, more restful sleep. Bonus: After a little practice, speed up this exercise by taking a mental inventory of where your body is holding tension and release it from just those muscle groups. You can do this technique anywhere!

As you know, exercise can be fun. If the idea of working out on sweaty gym machines doesn't thrill you or your eyes glaze over when you imagine walking or running, that's no excuse to be a couch potato. These days, there are tons of different ways to exercise. Many don't require expensive clothing or equipment. You can do them alone or with a friend. To name a few, try hiking; indoor rock climbing; tennis; ice skating; skiing; swimming; beach volleyball; aerobic classes; kickboxing; biking; skateboarding; martial arts such as karate, Tae Kwondo, Ju Jitzu; dance forms like ballet, jazz, modern, tap, and so forth; Zumba, yoga, and Pilates. Many teens swear by their Wii Fits. Whatever you do, do something. Just get moving. (Note: pressing keys on your computer doesn't count.)

Nourish

Just like cars, brains need fuel to run. Food provides that energy. So when you don't eat, you won't just feel sluggish and fatigued. Your brain won't work well, either. For example, neuroscientists have found that when people don't eat, the main brain structure involved in memory and learning is deprived of fuel and it's harder for people to learn. Based on this fact:

- **Eat breakfast**. Although mornings are hectic, it really *is* important to eat breakfast. A brand new study found that girls who skipped breakfast performed almost 10% worse on tests of attention, memory, and flexible thinking than those who ate. You don't have to make an elaborate omelet or pancakes with whipped cream and strawberries. But make sure you eat something that's high in protein, digests slowly in your system (so you're not starving by second period), and is low in sugar (so you don't crash as soon as it's metabolized in your system). Grab some healthy cereal, a handful of almonds, yogurt, a Lara bar (all natural, no additives or preservatives), string cheese, or peanut butter crackers. (Bonus: studies show people who eat breakfast regulate their weight better than those who skip breakfast.)

- **Maintain your blood sugar level**. Eat something healthy every few hours to keep your blood sugar—and therefore your mood and energy—on an even keel. This is especially important if you're prone to mood swings (highly common with hormonal fluctuations or stressful circumstances) or experience periods of sleepiness or spaciness during the day.

Your Mind

"To combat stress, I chill out after I finish eating lunch at school. I leave the cafeteria and walk around for awhile, which gives me a mental break from schoolwork."—Desiree

As you know by now, moderate or prolonged stress releases cortisol and messes up your thinking. As your body gears up for defensive action, you feel generally anxious and tense. Part of taking good care of yourself is reducing your stress and restoring your mind to a peaceful state. Use these proven techniques to clear out this toxic hormone:

* **Take a deep breath**. There's a scientific explanation for this old folk wisdom. When you breathe slowly and from your diaphragm (deep in your abdomen), you increase the oxygen in your blood. Your brain gets the message to stop producing stress hormones. Then your blood pressure and heart rate drop and you feel calmer instantly. Even better, you think more clearly. So breathing jump-starts the mechanism in your body that helps you recover from stressful or anxiety-inducing experiences. It's like dialing 911 and then saying, "Just kidding, I'm fine." This is a sure-fire way to regulate your emotions without medication.

* **Practice yoga**. Yoga, which combines breathing, gentle motion, and stretching, improves your strength and flexibility. But the benefits don't stop there. Practicing yoga regularly boosts the immune system, protecting you from getting sick, and also improves attention and focus. In fact, when it comes to stress, the mental perks of yoga—serenity, well-being, and centeredness—may even outweigh the awesome physical benefits.

* **Indulge yourself**. Be extra kind to yourself in stressful times. Wear your favorite cozy hoodie. Treat yourself to a little luxury. Give yourself a pedicure, get a manicure, or enjoy a scented, aromatherapy candle. Bubble baths with fragrant salts or bath bombs can be just as delightful for the spirit as for body.

Mindful Breathing Exercise

This technique, my personal favorite, quickly and effectively calms the mind, body, and spirit. The other great thing about it is that you can do it anywhere—sitting at your desk before a test, waiting for the dentist to start drilling, or willing yourself to sleep at night. Get in a comfortable position. Breathe in—slowly and deeply. When you breathe purposefully this way, you are deepening and slowing down your respiration, bringing more good oxygen to your mind and body. Concentrate on how the air feels as it enters and leaves your nostrils. When thoughts pop into your head, don't judge. Simply note them and then send them on their way, much like clouds float across the sky. Focusing on inhaling and exhaling, you're calming your entire nervous system. That's why mindful breathing is considered a great way to achieve serenity and peace of mind.

Guided Imagery Exercise

Close your eyes and think back to a time when you were completely relaxed. Maybe you were at the beach, on a sailboat, napping on a hammock, or on a picturesque mountain. Now try to recall everything about this blissed-out scene. Go through each of your senses and recall: What were you seeing? What colors do you remember? What did you smell? Was there salt in the air or the odor of freshly mown grass? What could you hear? People talking? Birds chirping? What did you feel: warmth, cold, dampness, or something soft against your skin? Could you taste anything? The more vivid your mental picture, the more powerfully you'll re-experience that same peaceful sensation. Whenever you need to relax, engage your senses and immerse yourself in this scene.

Your Spirit

"Spending time with people who love me and make me happy de-stresses me and gives me a better outlook."—Tina

"My parents take away my phone, but that's the only de-stressifying tool I have, because talking with a friend really helps."—Ginger

"Don't take stress out on family, friends, and loved ones. They're the ones that are there for you in the first place."—Thomasina

Connect with loved ones

As all these girls wisely recognize, infusing yourself with positive emotions is one of the best ways to de-stress and renew your energy and enthusiasm. That counteracts the sense of being overwhelmed and mentally exhausted. One of the best ways to do this is to connect with friends and family members who make you feel safe, secure, and loved. And by connect, I mean two ways: (1) *emotionally*—by being together, talking or doing activities and (2) *physically*—by touching (e.g., hugging, back rubs, tickling arms, etc.).

Researchers found that hugging eases stress—and just talking to a loved one helps almost as much. After a stressful experience, girls who hugged their mothers had lower levels of the stress hormone cortisol and higher amounts of the "love hormone" (oxytocin). Talking to their mothers on the phone rather than hugging them also reduced girls' stress, just not as powerfully. These studies prove scientifically why hugging friends or relatives not only makes you feel good, but also successfully lowers stress.

Another study showed that having a best friend with them protected kids from the negative effects of stressful experiences. When they had to go through stressful experiences without their best friend, researchers saw an increase in kids' cortisol—and you know what that does to the mind and body!—and a decrease in their self-worth.

All of us need relationships with people we value—and who value us. Taking good care of yourself requires being a bit choosy about who you hang with. Especially in times of stress, surrounding yourself with people who are kind, encouraging, and supportive helps. Their positive energy is infectious. By the same token, limit exposing yourself to chronically cranky, miserable, or complaining people. As you know, after awhile their negative energy starts to rub off on you and you start feeling just as blah.

As you know, certain friendships are stressful. Maybe you and your friend always get into fights, or she makes you feel bad about yourself. Sometimes so-called friends are too competitive or put you down. Or maybe she's unreliable, cancelling plans at the last minute when something better comes up. If you've been putting up with being treated badly, face the fact that this friend could be *adding* to your stress. Taking better care of yourself might require you to take action.

Maybe you can tell your friend how you feel. Although it was hard, *Casey* mustered the courage to tell her friend, *"When you make fun of me, it hurts my feelings and makes me think I can't trust you."* This friend kept apologizing, but then doing it again. So *Casey* decided she had to protect herself more by making a change. She said to this troublesome girl, *"This keeps happening, and it's really bothering me. I need to take a break from our friendship."* When Casey started hanging out with classmates who didn't tease or criticize her, she immediately felt happier and more relaxed.

Write Down Your Feelings

Tempted to flip out when someone ticks you off? Instead, write down your feelings. (Scientists say it's more satisfying to use pen and paper than a keyboard.) Then crumple the paper and toss it. The benefits? Studies show that using this simple strategy helps people sleep better and experience fewer negative emotions such as sadness. NOTE: The other benefit of paper and pencil over a keyboard is that you won't even be tempted to vent your anger in an email—and then impulsively press Send. This is hugely important because 99% of the time you'd regret it tomorrow. Plus, if that email were to be forwarded or go viral, you'd be in for some unbelievably major stress. Yikes!

See the humor

"Smiling, laughing, and a positive attitude really help me get through the day"—Liza

Having fun powerfully counteracts stress. When visiting schools, I'm thrilled to see girls comfortable enough to act silly with each other, chase each other down hallways, make stupid jokes, and laugh hysterically at nothing. Being joyful is great! Also, whenever you laugh or smile you release feel-good hormones that send messages to your brain that everything's okay. Those problematic stress hormones are called off.

Ask for help

"I wish girls knew it is okay to ask for help, especially from friends"—Wendy

Just recently, researchers found that people were able to reduce their fear and anxiety just by describing their feelings during stressful experiences. This is important because it suggests that if you hide your stress, you're not doing yourself any favors. Talking about feelings, especially with people you trust, actually helps. But it'll be hard to ask for help if you're trying valiantly to give the impression you've got it all together. Remember that while parents and teachers want you to do well, they also want you to be healthy and happy. So fess up if you're overwhelmed. Learning to express feelings appropriately—rather than, say having a hissy fit or picking a fighting with your sister—will come in handy with future college roommates, romantic partners, and bosses.

Can't Laugh? Try an Upbeat Chant

Research shows that positive thoughts lead to positive outcomes. Find a mantra that works for you. It can be anything from "I can do this" to "Everything's gonna be okay" to "God loves me." At first, say it when you're happy so your brain links the words to feeling good. Then, repeat your chant when you're stressed-out or upset and you'll calm down right away.

Ask for what you need. It's okay. It could be a small thing, like asking your mom to buy your favorite flavor of granola bar or yogurt. Or it could be something bigger, like telling your parents you want to go to a different school. Asking for help doesn't mean you'll get exactly what you want, but at least you'll express your feelings and start a conversation that can lead to finding real solutions.

Kendra's sassiness was getting her into a lot of trouble with her parents and older siblings. She was so stressed out by work and social stuff in school that as soon as she came home and someone said something she didn't like, she got snarky. Since she was one of five kids in her family, this happened pretty often! Plus, she had trouble concentrating on her work because she and her sibs all worked in the same room, which was too noisy for her. Kendra couldn't work in her own tiny bedroom, which had just enough space for her bed and dresser.

In therapy, Kendra and I talked about what could make the situation better. She told me that unlike her sisters and brothers, she needed more personal space. She craved alone time. Since she didn't think there was anything her parents could do, she had never spoken up. But with encouragement, Kendra talked to her parents. They squeezed a child-sized desk into her tiny bedroom, which made all the difference.

> ### 2-minute Relaxation Combo
>
> Remember the techniques you practiced earlier, rhythmic breathing and deep muscle relaxation? Well, now you're going to combine them—and also add another strategy. First get in a comfortable position. Start breathing deeply, remembering to inhale, hold, and exhale even more slowly. As you're doing this, mentally go through all your muscle groups head to toe, systematically relaxing them. If any area is especially tight, first tense your muscles before releasing them. Now, imagine yourself in your relaxing scene. The combo of imagery, rhythmic breathing, and deep muscle relaxation is guaranteed to make that stress melt away. You might even have to set an alarm clock!

Lastly, this advice comes from *Erin*: *"Sometimes it's okay just to let yourself stress out. I've always dealt with stress by letting it peak, and then it comes down naturally. It may take a day or an evening, but I thrive on knowing it will pass."*

CHAPTER SIX

Work Habits that Work for You

Earlier, we talked about the importance of creating sensible schedules. Although it's tempting to do tons of activities that make you feel busy and successful, hopefully you've left enough time to do your nightly homework and long-term projects while also studying for whatever tests and quizzes you have. Lots of girls tell me that while they struggle to keep up with endless piles of assignments, their classmates magically seem to get everything done. It may look that way, but everyone has to put in the time.

What separates girls who get it done (and even watch a sitcom or read a magazine before going to bed) and those who feel like they never catch up with their workload? Efficiency. You know how sometimes you spend hours on your assignments and get little done, while at other times you feel very productive because the work just flows? You can make this happen more often by keeping track of your assignments, organizing and monitoring your time, and staying focused.

If you're thinking, 'Oh, no, I'm terrible at those things!' have no fear. All these skills can be learned. You just have to figure out which approaches work for you and be willing to practice them. The payoff can be huge.

The Secret to Success

"When I'm stressed, I work harder. When the work is finished, the stress is gone."—Kay

Do you start out each semester with good intentions to stay on top of your work or improve your grades? But then, a few weeks into the new term, you feel discouraged by slipping back into old patterns. That's usually because you haven't actually changed your work habits. Unless you realize why things are staying the same, you might feel discouraged and hopeless. You can even lose your motivation. What I often hear girls say is, *"I can't possibly compete with the geniuses in my school who have perfect GPAs."*

The latest research pretty much shoots that excuse right out of the water. Fabulous students don't do well just because they were lucky to be born smart. It turns out that having a high IQ is only partly inherited. You can improve how well you think, reason, and solve problems by exercising your brain—for example, by reading, doing puzzles, and learning new things—much like building muscles when practicing sports. Scientists are basically saying we have some control over how brainy we are.

The even better news is that intelligence or IQ is only responsible for a very small part of success. Personal traits such as how motivated and self-disciplined you are, along with whether you have grit—perseverance—are four times more important than the intelligence you were born with. What does this mean? Those classmates of yours who look like geniuses are probably working harder than you think. Like *Biz Stone*, the co-founder of Twitter, has said, *"Timing, perseverance, and ten years of trying will eventually make you look like an overnight success."*

Procrastination

"The worst experience I had was in 8th grade. I had procrastinated so much that I had to finish the entire project in one night. I panicked and had trouble breathing. If it wasn't for my mother, I don't think I could have calmed down."—Alyson

A few years ago, when I did research for Stressed-out Girls, teens I interviewed gave me two main reasons for their stress: too much homework and not enough sleep. But these days, when I ask assemblies of girls about the biggest cause of their stress I hear about only one thing: Procrastination!

Instead of getting down to work when you get home from school or right after dinner, do you find a trillion "reasons" (read as: *excuses*) to put off opening your books? What I hear: *"I've got to clean my room before I can do anything else,"* or *"I'll just watch one show to relax first."* Most often, it's *"I've got to check my Facebook updates for a minute…."* That's a joke because you know what happens then: *"I got sidetracked by looking at everyone's pictures. Before I knew it, an hour had passed…"*

It's human nature to procrastinate. You probably do it when you're tired, when you don't feel like doing something, or when you're distracted. You put off tasks that are boring or hard or make you anxious. Or maybe you work yourself up when you think you can't do assignments perfectly. So instead you get involved in something more manageable—like rearranging paper clips or sharpening pencils. At least temporarily, you keep yourself from feeling scared, annoyed, or frustrated. Procrastination is just another word for avoidance!

The problem is that procrastination is a bad coping strategy. Even while you're engrossed in chatting with a friend or playing a computer game or shopping online, you're still aware of the task that's hanging over your head. Which only worsens your stress. And as soon as you face what you've still got to do, those same uncomfortable feelings return—with a vengeance. Only now you have even less time to do it, which adds to the pressure. Plus, procrastination can leave you feeling bad about yourself.

The good news is that you can work on procrastinating less. First, figure out the cause(s). Then find solutions that help. Use this mental checklist to decide what's making you put off what you'd be better off finishing now:

Sleepy? After a long day at school, you're probably tired (especially if you didn't get enough sleep this week). If possible, go ahead and take a quick power nap, like we discussed. But if that will turn into a 3-hour semi-coma, making you groggy for the rest of the day and keeping you awake all night, try these strategies instead:

- **Listen to upbeat music**. That'll perk you right up.
- **Switch your routine**. New and different experiences cause a rush of brain chemicals that make you more alert. If you usually sprawl across your bed when you work, sit cross-legged on the floor. Start off your homework in the dining room rather than your room.
- **Get active**. Physical movement will awaken you more than sitting still. Dance to upbeat music or take a 10-minute brisk walk, which will boost your energy for up to two hours. (BONUS: Taking your dog along might earn you brownie points with your parents.)

Hungry? Brains need fuel, especially when stressed. Avoid junk food, which may only make you sleepier. Instead, boost your brainpower with high protein snacks such as a handful of nuts, some cheese, hummus, or yogurt.

Mentally exhausted? Is your brain on overload?

- **Make a list**. Write down tasks and due dates in order of priority. Enjoy the feeling of accomplishment when you cross them off.
- **Pace yourself**. Alternate easy and hard tasks—or ones that require the most and the least amount of time.
- **Take breaks**. Play a quick game on your cell phone to have fun and activate brain cells. WARNING: Make that ONE game—or set your phone alarm to go off in 5 to 10 minutes.

   Too stressed?
- **Breathe deeply and exhale fully**. This will get rid of excess carbon dioxide so you get more oxygen to your brain and feel more mentally alert.
- **Work out.** Exercising in the early afternoon or up to two hours before bed lowers the stress hormone and increases feel-good endorphins.
- **Do whatever helps**. Spend 10 minutes doing whatever you know definitely relaxes you.

Cultivating Self-Discipline

While these strategies are all helpful, the bottom line is: To avoid procrastination, use self-discipline. That means making yourself do whatever you don't want to, whether that's getting out bed in the morning to go to school, doing your chores, flossing, or tackling your French conjugations. As you've just heard, the research is clear: the most successful, confident people aren't necessarily the smartest, but they're persistent and self-disciplined. They do whatever it takes to get the job done. The bonus? When you make yourself do something you'd rather avoid, you feel far more satisfied and better about yourself than when you procrastinate. Kudos!

Resisting Distractions

Speaking of self-discipline, the other challenge to getting work done is difficulty resisting distractions. I know, it's really, really hard to make yourself turn off your screens, stop chatting online with friends, and not check—much less respond to—incoming texts.

But here's what you should know:

- **Media use affects academic performance.** There's a clear connection between how much time you spend using media and your grades. In one large study, teens who were considered "heavy" users of technology were more likely to get fair or poor grades (mostly Cs or lower) than their classmates.

- **Multi-tasking is actually a myth.** Think you're good at doing your homework while watching YouTube, checking your news feed, and iChatting? Sorry, but you're not. No one is. You may be able to focus a little on each activity, but brain research proves you can't fully focus on anything. It's impossible to multi-*think*.

- **Distractions make you *less* productive and efficient.** Scientists have shown that when you switch your attention back and forth, it takes you 25% longer to finish tasks. Partly it's because the brain needs time to warm up every time you refocus, especially when tasks are challenging or brand-new. But also, if you're always busy, always doing *something,* you keep using up your storage of available energy until there's nothing left. Adults in the workplace who limit their access to email and texts are finding a huge jump in productivity. So would you!

What to DO

- Make a vow to yourself to avoid all screens while you're doing homework
- Before crunch times, consider what some girls do: They ask friends to change their passwords so they *can't* log onto Facebook and other tempting sites
- If you need the internet for studying, don't open Facebook, Tumblr, MySpace, Instagram, or any other social networking program on your computer
- Turn your cell phone on silent and put it across the room so you're not tempted to peek
- As *Caitlin* suggests, *"Let yourself check it as a reward for finishing a task."*
- Minimize intrusions; *Maddie* suggests, *"Tell parents that constant interruption for questions and stuff is the absolute worst. Save everything for a conversation when I'm done rather than busting through my door at their leisure!"*

> **Want to Boost Your Creativity?**
>
> ●——●——●
>
> A brand-new study by psychologists found that taking a break from technology and getting into nature may improve creativity. People performed better on a creativity test after backpacking for four to six days on a wilderness trip (without their devices) than they did before starting the hike. Can't think of a topic for your fiction assignment? Try going for a walk in the woods—and leaving your cell phone at home.

Finding Your Study Style

"Everyone works differently. You may work better alone, listening to music, taking a "Skype break" every 2 hours to laugh with friends."—Dani

Your parents may give you advice about how to study—for example, "Start your homework as soon as you get home from school," "Go up to your room, where it's quiet," or "Study your hardest subject first, when you're freshest." Or, they may say the opposite: "Warm up with your easiest subjects." These suggestions work for *them*. But studying isn't "one size fits all." Since everyone's needs are different, figure out what works best for you to make the most of your study time. Ask yourself these questions:

CHECKLIST: *What's Your Study Style?*

- Do you work better with last-minute, pressing deadlines, or when you give yourself plenty of time by starting way in advance?
- Do you get more work done alone, or with a partner or study group?
- With music on, or off?
- What kind of music helps you versus distracts you?
- Is it better to tackle your hardest subject first, when you're most energetic, or last, when you've gotten the easy stuff out of the way?
- Do you work best in a quiet area, or in a noisy place like the kitchen, library, or Starbuck's?
- Do you concentrate better in a messy workplace or in neat surroundings?
- Is it better for you to review material a bunch of times, or take careful notes the first time you read?
- Do note cards help you memorize?
- Before you write, do you make outlines, Venn diagrams, or flow charts?
- Does it help you to talk about your ideas before starting in on a paper?

Getting Organized

"When stressed, I like to make color-coded, categorized lists of what I need to get done because otherwise I'm stressed by not being able to remember what I need to accomplish."—Valerie

If you're constantly looking for where you put signed permission slips, the term paper that's due, or your coat, you're wasting valuable time. Trying to find something or calling a friend to ask about homework means another 5 or 10 minutes down the drain—and maybe points taken off your grade for lateness. Do people tell you to "pay attention to what you're doing" or to "stop being so scatterbrained?" If so, try these strategies to become better organized:

- Take a field trip to an office supply store to find a great planner. Explore all the different options until you find one you love.
- Then get in the habit of writing down *all* your assignments in *every* class *every* day. No exceptions!
- Before you leave school, mentally go through all your classes to make sure you bring home whatever you need. Or type up a checklist to post in your locker.
- Break down long-term assignments into manageable parts. Record in your planner exactly when you'll do each of the steps.
- Check your afterschool activity schedule to plan out when you'll do your homework. If you know you'll be busy, use free time during the day to get started.
- If time management is challenging, estimate how long each task will take you. Use a timer to check how much time it actually took. You'll soon get better at predicting and planning your assignments.
- At home, your motto should be, "A place for everything, and everything in its place."
- Use organizers to keep your school supplies neat and visible.
- At night, put all your homework and books in your backpack so it's ready to go.

Study Strategies

Just like organizational skills, study strategies have to be learned and practiced. Here are the practices that research suggests—and girls find consistently helpful:

- **Take good notes in class**. If it's hard for you to listen and write at the same time, or if you can't write fast enough to keep up, ask to compare notes with a friend so you'll get down everything important. If this is a constant struggle, talk to your guidance counselor. The school may be able to offer support for note taking.
- **Study in advance for tests**. Pretty much everyone agrees that the more you look at material, the better you'll learn it. You might be able to cram for simple memorization

tests, but deeper learning requires time. So before big tests, plan to do a little review every day.

* **Don't cheat yourself of sleep**. Remind yourself that research suggests you're better off choosing an extra hour of sleep over an additional hour of study. Scientists say sleep is especially needed for higher-level learning, such as putting together and applying complex information—essentially, what you do in school. (Believe it or not, studies have shown that people who pull all-nighters have the same—impaired—mental capacity as legally drunk individuals.)

* **Tackle difficult material right before bed**. In the past, common wisdom was do your hardest work right after school. But it turns out your brain can best process and remember information presented just before sleep. So do a quick review and it's light's out!

* **Study in different locations**. If you're used to doing all your studying in your room, consider new research that suggests you learn more effectively by studying in different places rather than in just one location—even when you study for the same amount of time. The more connections the brain creates, the easier it is to remember information.

* **Use active strategies**. Instead of just looking over your notes and rereading textbooks, actively explain concepts—to yourself, your parents, a classmate, even a sibling. The best way to learn is to teach.

* **Calming music can enhance learning**. Although teens are often told to turn off their music, some kinds don't distract—and actually improve focus and learning. It depends on tempo, content, and emotional tone. See the websites at the end of this chapter for some free downloads.

* **Stay well-nourished**. Remember that your brain needs fuel for peak performance. Aim for foods rich in protein, fiber, and complex carbs like oatmeal, which provide a steady energy supply.

* **Keep a positive attitude**. It's worth saying again: Being confident keeps you calm and focused, which leads to better performance. Remember *The Little Engine That Could?* Thinking that you'll succeed helps you succeed.

Tools to Use:
ONLINE RESOURCES FOR STUDYING MORE EFFICIENTLY

These websites have all been suggested by teens who find them helpful. Do you have others you like? Please let me know!

- **SelfControl.com**—free from Firefox add-ons website, this site warns you when you open time-wasting online pages

- **Stereomood.com**—the emotional internet radio that provides music especially for your moods & activities—for example, "happy," "working," "relaxing, "studying," "chillout," and "summer"

- **Rainymood.com**—offers nature sound, rain forest, sleeping noise, and sound therapy options

- **Quizlet.com**—free website for study games and making flashcards. Advertised as "The *best* way to study languages, vocabulary, or almost anything…"

CHAPTER SEVEN

Distracted By Problems

"Family drama related to divorced parents is in no way helpful to girls. Parents should keep it away from the children or make it better."—Chelsea

"I stress over my family. My dad has been struggling with finding a job, and my mom is an alcoholic/addict. I feel like I have to be successful to make up for the faults in my family. It's hard to enjoy my senior year."—Taylor

"I read every page five times and don't understand. It's like, 'What did I just read?'"—Anna

How well you can focus on school and extracurricular activities changes all the time. Sometimes you can give 100%, but at other times you're distracted. Not just for a moment, like when your crush walks by your classroom or you realize you forgot something important at home, but maybe for a day or a week or even a month. That's because you're preoccupied with problems. Your mind is elsewhere, making it hard to fully pay attention to what you're learning in class or supposed to be doing on your homework. When parents and teachers say to, "Just try your best!" they probably don't realize your "best" varies, depending on what else is going on in your life at the time.

Problems Big and Small

You could be dealing with—and dwelling on—an endless list of problems. Like Taylor and Chelsea, you may have pretty huge, stressful, and scary things going on in your family, like parents separating, divorcing, or going through hard times with their jobs, health, substances, or finances. Emma's mother drank too much after their father left. In class, she couldn't concentrate because she worried that her mother would crash the car while driving her younger sister to activities. Because of your family situation, your parents may not be around as much or be able to give as much attention and financial or emotional support as you'd like.

Maybe you're going through tough times personally. When Jocelyn became sick with Crohn's Disease, she felt nobody could possibly understand how her illness took over her life. You could be dealing with a traumatic experience like Nikki, who was sexually assaulted at a coed sleepover, or Elizabeth, who was abused for years by her uncle. Problems that are hard to talk about can be especially preoccupying and draining. Like Jess, whose father spent time in jail, and Emma, who wanted to keep her mother's alcoholism a secret, problems you're reluctant to share with your closest friends can weigh on you 24/7.

Hearing of upcoming changes in your family can also be hugely distracting. Maybe one or both of your parents are dating new people or announce they're getting remarried. You could be getting a new sibling, half-sibling, or slew of step-siblings. Perhaps you've just learned that you're moving. Or you're dreading your older sibling leaving for college. This kind of news can affect you more intensely than you'd have imagined. Remember, when you're already stressed it's that much harder to deal with more challenges. At least at first, thinking about what these family changes might mean can drain your attention away from everything else.

If you're thinking your problems aren't *that* bad, good! But even everyday stuff can distract you, temporarily making it hard to "do your best." *Julia*, for example, has been upset for days, ever since *"I overheard these girls saying my outfit was terrible, so now when I walk in the hallway I try to hide behind another group."* When your best friend is acting weird, maybe you can't stop dissecting your last conversation to figure out what could be going on. Or when the deadline to sign up for a dance nears, you obsess about who'll ask you—and whether it'll be in time.

Of course, it could be your BFF's problem rather than your own that's making you lose sleep. *Deb* told me, *"A really good friend of mine had sex with this random guy at a party the other night, even though we all begged her not to. He told all his friends, and now everyone in our school is talking about it. She's acting like it's no big deal, but it is."* When girls are worrying about friends who stop eating, start cutting themselves, skip classes, or talk about wanting to die, it's much harder to memorize vocab words or remember chemical equations.

And of course, romantic ups and downs are notoriously distracting. Breakups can be truly agonizing. Whether you're sad, furious, or just totally confused about what went wrong, it's still hard to focus on what your Spanish teacher is saying about past predicate tense. If your new ex happens to be in the same bio lab or lunch period as you, concentrating on anything besides where he's sitting and what he's doing may be next to impossible, at least for a while.

Problems *Do* Affect You

Many parents don't realize that the problems you have, big and small, affect your ability to do your "best." They may not connect family troubles with your difficulty concentrating, especially on school subjects that are mentally strenuous. Teachers also may not realize you can't work up to your usual standards because you're too worried about problems to think straight. They have no way of knowing your poorer test grades are due to the preoccupations that keep intruding whenever you try to study.

So what do parents and teachers usually think when they see a drop-off in grades? They assume you've stopped caring about your work. They may blame your friends, your boyfriend, or Facebook—even though they aren't the real (or only) cause. When adults get angry and punish you, you could feel worse. It's even harder to hit the books when situations seem unfair and you feel misunderstood. I often remind parents and teachers to consider other reasons for sagging grades besides lack of motivation or poor effort.

But it's even more important for *you* to realize—and accept—that problems can interfere with doing as well as you'd like. You can't do your best when your head is clouded by swirling thoughts and upsetting emotions. You can't expect to get devastating news and then just go about your business as if nothing had happened. You're human, not a robot.

When you can't do your work as quickly or as well as usual, don't get mad at yourself. That's the last thing you need when you're already distressed. Imagine your friend telling you that she's been so freaked out about her father's heart attack that she can barely think straight. Would you think she's being a drama queen? Would you expect her to forget about her father and just buckle down and do her work? Would you yell at her? So be just as courteous and understanding to yourself.

Getting Help

Accepting that problems can be distracting is the first step. Asking for help is the second. Remember, there is no shame in needing other people to support you through hard times. That's what relationships are all about. People who care about you will want to help you feel better. Don't worry if you're not comfortable telling them everything that's going on. You can just say you've got a problem that's troubling and distracting you. When you let your parents and teachers know this, it may help them to empathize with what you're going through, rather than jumping to unhelpful conclusions.

Here are some other people you may consider trustworthy and knowledgeable enough to talk to about problems:

- therapists
- medical doctors
- teachers
- guidance counselors
- religious leaders/clergy
- youth group directors
- camp counselors
- school administrators
- relatives (e.g., aunts, uncles, grandparents, cousins)
- friends' parents
- tutors
- mentors
- coaches

It's probably hard to know in advance who will be best to talk to. If at first you don't get the reaction or help you're looking for, don't give up. Keep reaching out until you find the right person.

Much as you'd like, it's unrealistic to expect people to solve all your troubles or make them go away. But some adults, like guidance counselors and school psychologists or social workers, are specially trained to handle problems like eating disorders, suicidal thoughts, and cutting among students. If you confide in them, they can take steps to start the process through which people get much-needed help. When friends are in real trouble, such as when health or safety is at stake, it's okay to break confidences. In fact, it's important to do that to save a life. That's not at all the same as blabbing a secret or starting a rumor. Plus, you can't deal with these sorts of problems on your own.

Even when people you confide in can't solve all your problems, it will make you feel better when they:

- listen attentively & respectfully
- empathize with your feelings
- validate your perceptions of the situation
- share their own, similar experiences
- offer specific advice
- refer you to other resources that can help
- relieve your burden of feeling responsible
- keep your secret confidential
- check in with how you're doing
- take steps to address problems

On Your Own

Along with getting help from other people, use the stress-reducing strategies you've learned so far to comfort yourself. Tell yourself exactly what you would say to your most treasured friend if she were in your situation. Use words of empathy, support, and encouragement like, "You're dealing with a lot right now," "Anyone would be upset and distracted," and "Give yourself a break." Focus on the positive to stay optimistic; there's no sense in dwelling on worst-case scenarios that may never happen.

Here are some other strategies that may reduce how much air time problems are taking up in your head:

❋ **Write in a journal**. Pour out how you're really feeling in a special, beautiful book. Psychologists say it's more useful to make sense of your experiences (e.g., why things might've happened) than just to vent. Also, try to include positive as well as negative emotions (ideally, four good things for every bad) to feel generally happier. (Note: Don't bear your soul in cyberspace, such as by posting private thoughts on Tumblr, which can lead to other problems.)

❋ **Draw**. If you like being creative (and remember, you don't have to be the next Picasso to enjoy art!), get out your paints, colored pencils, or crayons and draw whatever you're feeling. This is a great way to express your emotions and better understand yourself.

❋ **Write**. Many authors draw upon their own experiences, especially the difficult or dark ones, for creative inspiration. Write a poem or short story that conveys your troubles. Compose a song that captures your experience and resulting feelings.

❋ **Brainstorm solutions**. Dwelling on problems doesn't always lead to solutions. Try sitting down and jotting everything you can think of that might address your situation. When brainstorming, don't judge your ideas. Just keep generating ideas and be open to whatever comes up. Later, you can sift through them and decide which could be most helpful.

❋ **Schedule time to obsess**. Rather than trying to push troublesome thoughts from your mind, some mental health professionals advise setting aside specific times and places to think about them. Then preoccupations don't intrude at inconvenient times, such as when you're trying to work. Find 20 minutes or so to sit quietly, privately, and without interruption—and write your appointment with yourself in your planner to make sure it happens. See if thinking about your problems at that special time frees up your mind to focus better later on.

Remember, problems are a sucky, but inevitable, part of life. They can temporarily distract you from your goals and prevent you from being your best self. You aren't born knowing how to deal with them. It takes practice and the support of loving people to get through hard times. Meanwhile, be kind to yourself and use all the stress-reducing and comforting strategies at your disposal to feel better. The good news is that most bad times do come to an end.

CHAPTER EIGHT

The College Process—
Myths, Truths, and Strategies

"I'm a senior and this is my hardest year. I'm taking 3 extremely difficult classes, which next week, I have tests in all three of these classes on the same day. I am on a team, have a leadership role on the team, and one in my service organization. I have an extracurricular activity every day after school and don't get home until 7:30 PM. I am trying to apply to colleges, writing essays, and take the SATs this weekend. I'm averaging about 4 hours of sleep a night."—Gabi

#1 Goal: Keeping Stress to a Minimum

Just hearing the word *college* probably brings up a ton of thoughts and feelings. That makes sense. It's kind of a big deal to figure out where you want to spend four years of your life. It also may be daunting to think about living away from home, not seeing your family and friends every day, and leaving behind what's familiar. Change can be scary. Now add the stress of taking a bunch of standardized tests and filling out college applications to impress a committee of adults you don't know. All the while, you may be haunted by horror stories of kids who've been rejected from their favorite colleges or begrudgingly trudge off to their safety schools.

Like Gabi, you could let these college pressures take over until your junior and senior years totally suck. You could worry constantly about SATs, ACTs, and what you'll write about in your essay. You could dwell on not getting in anywhere good or, like many girls I speak with, not being accepted to the caliber of school that would make your parents proud. Obsessing about college could take up 95% of the airtime in your head, leaving little space for you to think about your passions, friends, or activities—if you even have time for them anymore...

But there's another option—the one I'd like to suggest. You can decide to go through the college process thoughtfully and sanely, keeping stress and fuss to a minimum. You can think of this time in your life as an adventure that can offer unexpected discoveries and build lifelong memories. You can use the college process to learn more about who you are and what you need to become your best self. You can trust in yourself and the universe that you'll end up in the place you are supposed to be—and that you'll be able to use all the strengths and skills you cultivated during the college process to thrive once you get there.

This is not some wild fantasy—it's totally doable. Admittedly, though, it's going to take effort on your part. You'll probably be around classmates and adults who talk nonstop about what schools are looking for, how to raise SAT scores, Early Decision versus Early Action, etc. Friends may get weird, either obsessing about college 24/7 or acting like you need security clearance even to find out where they're applying. Some people freak out. But whatever happens, you can resist getting caught up in the hype and hysteria. Here's what you need: the myths and truths about college, tips for maintaining a healthy attitude, and strategies for going through this process sensibly.

The Basics

These guidelines can help keep the college process manageable:

- **Make a plan**. It's sensible to plan out in advance the high school classes you'll take, which standardized tests you'll do, and when you'll take them. That way, you won't be unprepared or have to rush to fulfill requirements at the last minute.

- **Follow a sensible timeline**. Unless you go with older sibs on college visits or pass by schools on family travels, you don't need to start until junior year. Many girls who've visited colleges as freshmen or sophomores tell me (1) it made them more stressed-out and overwhelmed, and (2) they didn't remember much about the schools when it came time to apply.

- **Visit Colleges**. Get a feel for different campuses as a junior or senior. Vacations are a good time so you don't miss too much school. But college should be in session so you get a sense of the student population and culture. Depending upon distance from home, you may not be able to visit all schools before applying. But before sending in any college deposit, make sure you spend time on campus at least once, preferably for an overnight visit.

❋ **Focus on high school**. Don't get so caught up in college apps that you lose sight of what's going on now. Keep up with your work and extracurriculars so you don't get behind. Also, remember to have fun with your friends. You'll all be going off to college soon.

❋ **Cap the College Talk**. To avoid constantly having to talk—or answer parental questions—about college, make an agreement to limit discussions. An educational advisor I know recommends setting aside a specific time—for example, from 4 to 5 PM on Sundays. That way, most nights you can talk about current events or sports or "Girls" during dinner without worrying that you'll be asked for an update on the status of your apps or SAT practice tests.

Debunking Myths

To get off on the right foot, let's get rid of the most common misconceptions about college:

#1) **There's a perfect school for you**

Why it's not true:

❖ First of all, there's no such thing as a perfect school, just like there's no perfect friend or teacher or roommate or romantic partner or career. All have pros and cons. Knowing that there's actually no single school out there that's perfect for you should ease some of the pressure…

❖ There are many, many fine colleges. Although you may feel desperate to go to one school, there are others out there where you could be just as happy and equally, if not more likely, to thrive. You just may not know about them yet.

❖ Unless you're 100% sure, don't apply Early Decision. Jenna always dreamed of going to BU. But when she revisited schools in April after getting acceptance letters, she fell in love with GW, majoring in political science and settling there after graduation with a good job offer. It was a good thing she had decided not to apply ED.

#2) **Where you go to college determines your entire life**

Why it's not true:

- Many successful adults never went to college, dropped out, or graduated from schools nobody ever heard of.

- "Name" or prestigious schools may get you in the door for an initial job or internship interview, but that's as far as it gets you. After that, it's up to you to prove yourself.

- It's not where you go to college that matters, but rather *what you do once you get there*. Making the most of all your opportunities is what shapes your life.

#3) **Raising your SAT or ACT scores is the key to getting into college**

Why it's not true:

- Many girls taking SATs or ACTS think, "The next few hours are going to determine my whole life." A more stress-inducing—and self-defeating—thought would be hard to imagine. Or a falser one. Your scores are not the be-all and end-all. If you do well, congrats! If not, it doesn't mean *you're* not great. This test measures a certain kind of reasoning under specific conditions. It doesn't measure different kinds of intelligence, creativity, talent, social skills, maturity, perseverance, leadership, and all the other personal qualities that *really* lead to success.

- The SAT and ACT scores colleges list are averages—meaning that some students have higher scores and others have lower scores. These tests are only one of many criteria colleges use to select students. So don't let disappointing scores dissuade you from applying to a school you really love.

- Making yourself crazy to raise your SATs or ACTs is not a good plan. Schools routinely reject plenty of applications with perfect scores. They look for a variety of qualifications and talents to build the most interesting and diverse incoming freshman class. In fact, more and more colleges either don't require standardized tests or make them optional. Ask your guidance counselor for a list.

- If the thought of taking SATs or ACTs stresses you out, consider this. Cutting-edge research is showing that people who tend to be worriers (often the smartest individuals, btw!) can train themselves to do well on stressful, high-performance tasks. The key is to remember that a *little* stress is actually good because it helps you to focus and think sharply. Inoculate yourself against the negative effects of *too much* stress (e.g., brain freeze) by taking lots of practice tests while using the exercises described earlier to keep your stress level low.

AMAZING FACT: Research shows that when students taking standardized tests for graduate school were told that anxiety would make them do better, they scored 50 to 65 points higher. Hearing that the jitters could benefit them didn't lower their anxiety. What caused their scores to soar? Their positive state of mind, which boosted oxygen flow and energy in their brains. So if you start to panic mid-test, remember the excitement you felt during a competitive soccer or softball game or the thrill of performing in a jazz recital or piano competition. Channel that feeling!

Crying Over 20 SAT Points

Too often, I've seen girls freak out when friends beat them by 20 or 30 SAT points. This is just silly. First off, a measly 30 SAT points isn't going to determine whether you're accepted or rejected to a college. Second, statistically this difference in scores is totally meaningless. It's within the same range.

#4) **To get into your dream school, work your butt off and do everything right**

Why it's not true:

- First of all, there's no such thing as "doing everything right." As we've already discussed, you can't possibly do everything, and you can't do everything right. Moving on…

- These days, if you make the most of your high school years and do well, you earn the privilege of entering the college lottery. Whether you get into your dream school is a total crapshoot.

- Admissions committees say they could fill each incoming class with perfectly qualified applicants. What determines why one is accepted and another is rejected? Who knows? Maybe they need majors in East African women's literature or someone from the mid-Atlantic states who plays glockenspiel in the marching band.

- In other words, since college admissions are likely to remain mysterious, it's better to focus on doing your best, learning how to learn, and figuring out what you love so you can make the most of college, wherever you go.

Developing Your List

If you're choosing schools based on *U.S. News and World Report* rankings, the "most competitive" sections of college handbooks, or prestige (e.g., Ivy League), my suggestion would be: Stop! If you remember only one thing, please make it be this: WHAT MATTERS IS NOT THE COLLEGE, BUT RATHER THE *MATCH* BETWEEN YOU AND THE COLLEGE.

Here's an example of what I mean. Anya and Bethany are both strong students who want to be writers. Anya has her heart set on going to a well-known Ivy League university that boasts well-published faculty members and high acceptance rates to graduate school programs. But Bethany is leaning toward a small, liberal arts college. She thinks she'll do better in smaller classes working directly with professors rather than teaching assistants. And while Anya thrives on competition, Bethany is too anxious to speak up when she feels intimidated by her classmates. She's drawn to a school that is known for its collaborative community. Fortunately, these girls choose different routes to becoming writers based on their own learning styles and needs.

That's why knowing yourself is the most crucial part of the college process. You have to know what you need to be successful, where you'll fit in, and what appeals to you. Consider these factors:

- **Cost**. Although you may not immediately think of finances, it's a good thing to discuss with your parents before you get too far into the college process. Learn the realities: What can your family afford? Should you attend a state university? Will your choice of college affect whether you'll need loans or scholarships? Should you consider the cost of travel if you like schools far from home? If you nail this down first, money is less likely to be a bigger stress than it has to be.

- **Location**. Many girls have opinions about where they want to go to college. Not just the location (e.g., East Coast, West Coast, the South), but also how far away from home they want to be. But make sure you're not making long-term decisions based on short-term reactions (e.g., "Get me as far away from my annoying parents as possible" or, the opposite, "My boyfriend and I want to stay together, so I'm applying to the same school"). Remember, you don't need physical distance to feel emotionally separate and grown up. Being an hour away from home can give you the experience of living in a different world.

- **Urban versus rural**. Depending upon where you grew up, what makes you comfortable, and what you want to experience, you may have your heart set on the high energy, diversity, and cultural opportunities of a city or the serenity and seclusion of a rural college that is its own community. You may have strong opinions about the benefits of a traditional campus, wherever it's located.

- **Climate**. This is a hot issue—no pun intended—that can also gets a lot of play. If you absolutely can't live without skiing, it makes sense to apply to northern schools near slopes. If you're always cold or hate chilly weather, being somewhere warm seems wiser. But unless you have strong needs, other criteria should be a higher priority. Once you're absorbed in your new college life, you might notice the weather less than you might think.

- **Size of school**. Consider how student body size affects you both academically and socially. Do you want personal attention and/or support offered more by smaller colleges? Are you looking for a larger or more diverse pool of classmates and potential friends? Do you want a university that offers particular majors or different courses of study if you change your mind? Is school spirit or athletic events important to you?

- **Extracurricular opportunities**. Even if you don't complete on the college level, you may want to continue rowing, ice skating, or playing club lacrosse. Or maybe you want to learn to be a bartender or take up Tae Kwondo or play piano just for fun. To learn about school clubs and social events, ask current students and check out bulletin boards in dorms and student unions when you visit colleges.

- **Student body**. One of the best ways to evaluate colleges is to decide if you can imagine yourself there. That's one reason why campus visits are so crucial. You won't need advice on this. Chances are, you'll know this soon after arriving at a school and looking around. Pay close attention to your gut feeling—or, as I like to call it, your wise inner voice.

- **School culture**. Like the two aspiring writers described earlier, you have to figure out what sort of environment is best for you. If you've struggled in high school, you may choose a less competitive college. You may want to be with classmates who value balanced lives of social interaction and extracurricular activities along with study. Or, you may crave being around intense students whose idea of socializing is having long, intellectual debates at all hours of the night. This is why it's so crucial to know yourself.

- **Availability of support**. If you've struggled with learning or emotional challenges, give lots of thought to what sort of support you may need in college. You may be tired of getting help and prefer to do it alone, but it's good to know there are services there just in case, especially during the transition of freshman year, Many schools claim to offer academic and psychological support, but do the research to be sure they have exactly what you're looking for. If in doubt, visit the appropriate departments to discuss your needs before you send in the deposit.

"My brother is a freshman @ Notre Dame, so I'm being pressured by my parents to go there. My number one is a school that I feel better suits my personality. What should I do?"—Michaeline

Just as crucial when you're figuring out college stuff is remembering what is NOT important:

- Where your sister(s) or brother(s) went to college
- Where your mother went to college
- Where your father went to college
- Where your grandparents went to college
- Where your friends apply to college

Dealing with Parents

Hopefully, you have parents who are interested and attentive when you talk about college, but don't bug you endlessly about every step of the application process. Ideally, they support your dreams, whatever they are, instead of burdening you with fulfilling theirs. But as you well know, in real life this doesn't always work out perfectly. Many girls tell me about loving, caring mothers and fathers who mean well but actually cause more stress than they alleviate. Now is the time to have honest, direct conversations to express your real feelings, negotiate solutions, and resolve differences.

These are the most common situations I hear about and some thoughts about how to deal with them:

- **Specific, narrow goals**. The more parents think you should have a certain GPA, SAT score, or focus on a single college, the more stress you're likely to suffer. After all, narrow goals don't give you much wiggle room to please them—or yourself. This is probably the most challenging problem for girls. Keep reminding yourself that the process of becoming successful in life can follow many different paths. Find role models who have been creative or untraditional in finding their way. Use resources such as guidance counselors, college advisors, and trusted relatives to be the voices of reason with parents who have one-track minds.

- **Unreasonable expectations**. Since your parents adore you and think the world of you, they may think you're capable of doing anything and everything. This, however, is most likely a gross exaggeration. Everyone has limitations. Try as you might, maybe you can't ace physics, score in the 99th percentile on the

SATs, or get into the one school your parents have their hearts set on, any more than you can grow another foot. Overestimations of your talents can be a huge burden. This is another time to call upon other supportive adults.

CONSIDER THIS: Are your parents' expectations as unrealistic as you think? Many girls never check out whether their assumptions are right. For example, *Belinda* recently became distraught when her older brother got into an Ivy League school. *"They're going to be so disappointed when I don't get in there in three years, and they'll be too embarrassed to put my school's sticker on the car!"* she cried. A few weeks later, when Belinda invited her mother to her therapy session, she heard a far different perspective. Apparently, Belinda's mother never imagined she would apply to that college because it "wasn't for her." Because Belinda is so active and involved in school clubs, she thought a school with more diverse social and extracurricular opportunities would be better.

- **Anxiety**. Because parents want the best for you, they desperately hope you'll be happy. Watching you go through the college process probably makes them uneasy. Some can keep it under control more than others. Unfortunately, if your mother or father is high-strung, it's probably going to stress you out more. Keeping discussion to a minimum can help. Also, if you assure them that you're on top of things as you go along, they may worry less.

- **Expert advice**. Many parents think they're experts in this area because at some point they went to college. But so much has changed since then that their advice is likely outdated. With the competition today, many parents wouldn't even get accepted their own alma maters. They may look down on excellent schools that didn't have good reputations in the past. If you're unsure of your parents' advice, get other opinions—not just from guidance counselors and college advisors, but also kids who recently graduated who can give you the real scoop.

- **Micromanaging**. For lots of reasons, some parents try to oversee every step of the college process—or take over completely. They even say, "*We're* thinking of applying…" But it's important for *you* to take ownership. It's *your* college experience. Demonstrate that you're capable of planning everything out and meeting deadlines. Then you can say, "Thanks, but I've got it under control." Besides, this is good practice for when you're juggling classes, social events, clubs and activities, studying, eating, sleeping, and doing laundry on campus. *Sara* suggests, *"Make the college process fun by planning a college application* *night. One easy, fun way to fill out college applications is to have girls get together one night and do them in a sleepover."*

- **Too much tutoring/prepping**. Again, in the hope of giving you every advantage, many parents sign up for SAT prep courses, private math tutors, writing coaches, and other expensive, time-consuming programs (sometimes starting in freshman year). But this can make you feel overwhelmed—and also worse about yourself. *Marge* asks, *"Aren't I okay the way I am?"* Talk with your parents about the kind of support that seems right for you. But appreciate whatever programs or sessions they're giving you by doing assigned work and benefitting as much as possible.

CONSIDER THIS: Although your parents may not be experts on college, they do know a lot about *you*. In fact, they've known you longer than your guidance counselor or college consultant have. So don't roll your eyes or tune out when they offer advice. Be receptive to hearing their perspective on what you need to blossom in college, even if you don't agree with everything they say.

Campus Visits

Researching schools online, reading college handbooks, and speaking to knowledgeable people are a great first step, but nothing substitutes for experiencing campuses first-hand. So what should you do to make sure you get the most out of your visits?

- **Prepare**. It's good to think beforehand about what you'll focus on because there will be a lot to see and take in. What will give you the most useful information: Sitting in a classroom? Eating a meal in the student union? Hanging out in the dorms? Talking to a coach? Meeting with a professor in the department of your intended major? Experiencing Greek life? It's good to have a variety of experiences while you're there. Insure you get to talk to the people you'd like by calling or emailing ahead to make appointments.

- **Carve out space**. To form your own, unbiased opinions, make an agreement with anyone who comes with you on visits (parents, friends, siblings, etc.) not to discuss impressions right away. After the visit, jot down your thoughts, even if you think you'll remember them, since memories can blur (especially on whirlwind tours of multiple colleges within a few days) Later on, you can compare notes.

- **Info sessions**. You might hear some important things you didn't already know about the school's philosophy and mission, student culture, new programs or departments, or abroad opportunities. Some students say all info sessions sound alike, but decide for yourself how useful they are. Alternately, you can look around a campus on your own before going to an info session or asking for an interview.

- **Campus tours**. Guided walks around campus are a great way to get a feel for the place—except for one thing. Too often, girls tell me their opinions of schools are completely swayed by the student guide. All it takes is someone annoying, weird, nerdy, or in some way off-putting to make you cross a college off your list. Try to keep some perspective here, girls. A tour guide is only one student out of hundreds or thousands. Plus, the opinions of one person don't represent those of the entire school community. Go to the library or cafeteria and talk to other, random students, or contact family friends or students from your high school who go there. One way or another, check out a school further before letting one student crush your interest.

- **Gut feelings**. On the other hand, first impressions can be powerful. When you pull up to campus, you may instantly think, "I can totally see myself here" or the opposite, "Get me out of here ASAP!" This vibe can be based on something you notice about how students look or act. Other times, you may not have a clue where your gut feeling is coming from or how to explain it. If after driving three hours you take one look out the window and refuse to set foot on campus your parents might be mystified or exasperated, but it's important to honor your inner voice.

- **Have fun**. Make sure college visits are enjoyable. Whatever tensions exist between you and your parents, set them aside. This may be a once-in-a-lifetime chance for a road trip. Take time out for detours to random places you'd otherwise never see. Make it an adventure you'll remember forever—and have a blast.

Personal Statement/College Essay

Although the college essay has become infamously stress-producing, it doesn't have to be. Here are a few tips:

- **Be yourself**. This should be your primary, if not only, goal. Instead of aiming to impress, think about writing about something that is 100% authentic. A good college essay requires telling a uniquely personal story in your own voice. Whether it's serious, amusing, ironic, or self-deprecating, it has to be *you*.

- **Pick a topic**. Write about what you really and truly care about, intrigues you, made a huge difference in your life, moves you in some way, or taught you an important lesson. It could be an idea, a person, an experience, or a place. As long as it's meaningful to you.

- **Avoid clichés**. If someone advises you to write about a hardship or medical condition you've suffered because "this is what college admissions committees want," please think twice—no, three times. Unless this issue genuinely resonates with you, forget it. Your heart has to be in your essay or you'll dread writing it and the tone will end up sounding false.

- **Think small**. Forget global warming or world peace. Focus on an everyday experience that meant something to you. Some of the best essays I've ever read were about seemingly mundane topics: being benched an entire high school basketball season; researching a parent's family tree; meeting a homeless person; fulfilling a promise to one's hairdresser; and conquering a lifelong fear of bicycles. What made these essays so special—absorbing, poignant, funny, heartwarming, or revealing—was their authors' ability to tell stories in ways that faithfully and convincingly conveyed who they were.

- **Get feedback**. Every good writer needs an editor. Ask someone or several someones you trust to give you feedback on the content, tone, style, and mechanics of your essay. Edit and then edit some more. When proofreading, read it backwards to make sure you don't overlook mistakes.

Acceptances and Rejections

Waiting to hear back from colleges, whenever that happens, can be nerve racking. Hopefully, it'll all go as you wish and you'll be happy with your opportunities. Even so, you may have lots of different feelings, some of which may surprise you. Many girls expect to be thrilled by getting into their ED school, but then second guess their choice. Others imagine being devastated by a rejection from a favorite college, only to feel a sense of relief. Give yourself permission to accept whatever you feel. You can learn key things about yourself. A few potential situations to manage:

- **Being happy when friends are upset**. It's perfectly okay to share your good news even when friends are unhappy, just as you'd expect them to do if the situation were reversed. Hiding your feelings could even make things awkward and distance you from close friends. Just remember to check in with them to see how they're doing, too.

- **Being upset when friends are happy**. Ideally, when good friends get into college, you want to be excited for them. But if they're sporting sweatshirts with their new college names emblazoned on them while you're scrambling to fill out additional applications, you may not feel as thrilled as you'd like. That doesn't make you a bad person. In fact, it's normal to experience a mixture of different feelings, even envy or resentment at what you might see as their good luck (maybe undeserving!). Give yourself time to absorb and process your feelings.

- **Parental disappointment**. Sometimes I hear that girls feel more upset about their parents' disappointment than their own. *Leeanne* says, *"Not getting into college Early Decision was a double disappointment because I knew my mother would be devastated, too."* In this case, keep in mind that your parents are disappointed *for* you, not *in* you.

- **Maintain perspective**. After working with teen girls for more than 30 years, I am convinced that rejections are a clear sign that something is not meant to be. You may not know the reason just then—or ever. But trust that this particular school(s) is not part of your journey. It's not a tragedy, though it may temporarily feel like one. You will go to another college where you'll thrive, make lifelong friends, and become part of a community that will be lucky to have you.

When *Evi* came back to see me during her first Christmas break, she said, *"I didn't think so at first, but getting rejected everywhere but my safety was the best thing that ever could have happened. I never imagined coming here, but I ended up exactly where I should be."*

APPENDIX

De-Stressing Your School Environment

Some girls have made lasting changes in their schools that reduce stress for everyone. They've worked with teachers, guidance counselors, school psychologists, and administrators to help them to better understand what it feels like to be a student these days. Their committees came up with tangible ways to make their schools less pressured, more supportive, and fun to be around. Implementing even one or two of these strategies can make a real difference to your school's culture. If you're interested in taking a next step, here are some ideas I've learned from teens around the country:

- Reduce assignments of busy work
- Limit the number of exams given on a single day
- Minimize homework given over weekends
- Eliminate class rank
- Stop making honor rolls public
- Don't publish lists of colleges seniors will attend
- Institute homework-free holidays
- Reduce homework assignments during summer vacations
- Paint serene murals on walls in school lobby and/or cafeteria
- Make a special room or lounge available for students to rest quietly/meditate
- Offer yoga and/or meditation as gym electives

- ❈ Invite local massage therapy students to offer free neck massages during lunch
- ❈ Make a "Rejection Wall" in the guidance office where college applicants can post their letters (adding humor and taking away the shame of rejection)

Do you have other suggestions? What have you accomplished in your school to reduce stress and make the environment friendlier/more supportive?

I would love to hear your thoughts and ideas, which I will gratefully pass along to other girls eager to reduce their stress.

email@ronicohensandler.com

Thank you!

www.ingramcontent.com/pod-product-compliance
Lightning Source LLC
Chambersburg PA
CBHW041437040426
42453CB00021B/2451